# FUNDAMENTALS OF ROUTESETTING

LOUIE ANDERSON

# Fundamentals of Routesetting

ISBN# 978-0-9766630-1-0



Printed in China



All uncredited photos by the author.

Front cover: Setting at Vital Climbing Gym – Bellingham, Washington

Contact the Author: **Louie Anderson**

PO Box 411, Silverado, CA 92767-0411 - louieanderson@live.com

## CLIMBING AND ROUTESETTING IS DANGEROUS!

The user of this book accepts all risks associated with the activities described herein. Climbing and routesetting carries great risk for injury or death. The information offered in this book shall in no way supercede one's own judgment and/or common sense when it comes to assessing the dangers involved in ANY situation. The author, editors, publishers, and any of their agents accept no liability for any injuries incurred from using this book or participating in any of the activities described herein.

# Fundamentals of Routesetting

Louie Anderson

with

Competition Organization by Scott Rennak

and

Topical essays by internationally acclaimed routesetters

Vince Schaefer

# Contents

# Acknowledgements

This book is by no means solely my own effort. The following individuals and groups have contributed greatly in one way or another. As such, I would like to publicly acknowledge and thank the following:

*Chris Danielson* – For your friendship and the countless conversations we've had over the years about all things regarding holds and setting. Also for writing the Foreword and supporting this book project. Your efforts to legitimize setting activities in the US and abroad have paved the way for the next generation of routesetters.

*Scott Rennak* – For your vision in bringing bouldering competitions towards where they are today with the your original competition series that became the ABS. Thank you also for once again handling the chapter on competition organization.

*Laura and Alex Bennet* – For once again helping to present my ramblings and ideas in a beautifully designed layout.

*All of the setters who wrote essays for this book* – Your insight helps us all to look at the activity of setting through different eyes and inspires us to do better. Thanks for your contributions.

*Anyone who has presented routesetting info in the past* – Until this book you who have taken the time to write on the topic or share your wisdom through clinics and other training methods have gotten routesetting to the point it is today. Your thoughts and the ensuing variations and implementation by other setters have helped to form the consensus opinions offered in this text. Without your efforts, we'd all still be making it up as we went.

*All climbing gym owners* – without your dreams, and the gyms that embody those dreams, there would be no need for setters; or for this book. Thanks you for giving us a forum in which to practice our craft.

*All the photographers who allowed their images to be used* – Your images capture indoor climbers enjoying setting's final product: the climbs themselves. They also break up what would have been a bunch of dense text. When we were kids, we liked books for the pictures found in them and often looked at all the pictures before reading the text. I'm sure this book will be no exception.

*All the advertisers who supported this project* – Please take the time to look at their advertisements (starting on page 207) and support the companies that helped to make this book possible.

And finally,

*Valarie* – Not only is she my partner in life, but also my partner at The Factory Bouldering, our gym, where we place the highest importance on offering our climbers the best setting we can. I love you.

*Vince Schaefer*

Caroline Treadway

# FOREWORD

Almost 20 years ago, after an Outward Bound course in Colorado, I became inspired to climb. Back where I was from in western New York, there was not much rock close by and there were no indoor gyms. But there was an exterior cobblestone wall that lined the outside of a local hardware store and my friends and I would go there in the evenings and traverse back and forth or do a few moves up and down the 10 foot wall. I think of this as my first routesetting experience. I still distinctly remember making up eliminates to increase the climbing challenges and getting excited whenever I completed one.

Flash forward about a decade and I had gained more substantive experience actually attaching modular climbing holds to artificial walls designed for climbing, routesetting at a few different gyms around the country and for many competitions. I had also gotten involved with the American Bouldering Series, and it was around this time that I came to know Louie Anderson. Louie was one of the most recognized and respected routesetters in the Southern California community. He had a reputation as a prolific hold shaper, developer of sport-climbing areas, and expert climbing wall builder. Always interested in learning whatever I could from others in the industry, I got a copy of Louie's original book "The Art of Coursesetting," and read through it eagerly in a single sitting. It was the only writing on the subject that I had ever encountered and though I had many years of experience, I was excited again by the well-organized presentation of fundamental concepts, informative personal essays, and competition planning resources. I immediately wished I had this book ten years earlier when I first became interested in creating climbing movement and my own routesetting career began developing.

I have come to know Louie even better personally in the years since, routesetting for a couple events in California and talking with him countless times about our shared passion for plastic. Louie's writing on routesetting, his seemingly limitless number of artistic hold creations, and his friendship have continued to inspire my ideas about climbing and the craft of building movement. A lot has changed since either Louie or I began playing with climbing walls and holds and the quick pace of change in the industry always keeps me reflecting on the past.

Climbing is intriguing to many in part because it can be defined, engaged in and explored in so many diverse ways. Over the past century the history of various disciplines of climbing has evolved and the activity, sport, or art of climbing, however you choose to define it, constantly mutates, shifts, and expands. But there is something more basic that shapes and drives this diversity and its evolving nature. Whereas running and swimming, to take two examples, are basic human acts of form and fitness where individuals push themselves to greater limits of strength and endurance to improve their time or accomplish a greater distance, climbing is different. Though it is a similarly elementary human act, climbing is infinitely more *creative*. Climbing, as we understand it, bends and adjusts with time precisely because climbers are explorers and creators, always molding and re-forming what climbing is. We create new challenges for ourselves constantly.

Mountaineers first began trying to find a way to the top of a new peak by creatively searching for the most accessible path and developing methods, tools, and equipment to do so. When just getting to the top was not enough, they had to find new routes that were more challenging. It is the same for all other disciplines of climbing and the evolution of each. Climbing on artificial walls developed initially for training but very quickly became popular as a recreational and fitness activity. In this way, climbing morphs, stretching out in new directions as we imagine and explore new terrain. Those who participate in each of the different aspects of climbing all engage in their own creative challenges, but the factors that shape and form each are always similar. Put simply, *we all go up.*

In the 25 years since the first artificial climbing walls in North America were being fastened together, the growth of artificial wall climbing as its own unique form of climbing has been rapid and intense. Today, the vast majority of new climbers experience climbing for the first time at their local artificial wall and many come to understand and identify themselves as climbers mostly, or even sometimes exclusively, through their experiences indoors. At the same time, routesetting as a craft has evolved just as much in the years since the original publication of Louie's "The Art of Coursesetting" as it had over the entire first two decades of the climbing wall industry.

Routesetting is the most essential creative aspect of what we understand indoor or artificial wall climbing now to be. In this way, routesetting embodies the spirit of climbing and Louie's writing on the subject does the same. The act of creating vertical paths by attaching modular holds on a blank wall involves all of the same elements that any other discipline of climbing does – curiosity, creativity, technique, problem solving, and the desire to challenge, or even to inspire. And thus the craft of routesetting is part of the broader history and evolution of climbing itself; we all go up. The difference with artificial wall climbing is that without routesetters building movement, there simply is no up.

Routesetting, like climbing, is not easy, neither to do nor to explain. Articulating information about basic mechanics and theories about what is such a creative, complex and mostly independent act, especially in writing, is a difficult task. In "Fundamentals of Routesetting," Louie has crafted an accessible yet detailed follow up to his original work, updated with new content and essays from a diverse group of experienced routesetters. Whether you are a climber building a home wall interested in learning about how to set for your own training, or working full-time as a routesetter in a commercial climbing gym, there is always something more to learn. As Jacky Godoffe, the legend of Fontainbleau and a great influence in competition climbing taught me, there is no absolute truth to routesetting, but only many different ways to explore it.

Aside from being a fun and imaginative act, routesetting is also now seen as a possible vocation for young and creative climbers with a passion for artistic expression, problem solving, and what is fundamentally climbing product design. With so many new walls being built worldwide, the importance of routesetters as craftsmen of climbing only increases with each new route set. As the climbing wall business grows this industry needs more climbing professionals, as we are the ones who create, present, and shape this new aspect of climbing. This is all the more reason why this new book is a valuable reference tool both for individual routesetters and for the climbing wall industry as a whole. "Fundamentals of Routesetting" provides a comprehensive introduction to those interested in learning where to begin, and provides a wealth of useful technical information and motivation to those who have been routesetting for many years. We may all explore this book and this craft in different ways, just as we each explore our own ever-evolving climbing experience. Routesetting, as an act of self-expression, a craft, or a career, is always growing and evolving – as we all go up.

**Chris Danielson**

*Owner, Thread Climbing, LLC*

*Chairman, USA Climbing Routesetting Committee*

*IFSC Routesetter*

Vince Schaefer

# PREFACE

While I primarily consider myself an outdoor climber, I've spent a fair amount of time over the years watching the evolution of indoor climbing. From the painful, first generation artificial holds and vertical to horizontal roof "gyms" to the present incarnation, I've enjoyed it all. One of the things that has always appealed to me is the setting of routes and boulder problems. In the old days anyone who showed an interest was given a set of wrenches and allowed to throw up some holds. Initially it was all about setting hard climbs. The spoken goal was to create training routes, but more often than not the real intent was to make your friends suffer.

Obviously, this approach did little to attract new gym users and many of the first small gyms went under. There was no real awareness or history to follow when it came to attracting and subsequently catering to new clientele. No one really had the experience to teach anyone else how to set climbs, and there were certainly no resources to refer to. Because those of us setting the climbs were to a certain extent making it up as we went, real progress and education in setting took quite a while to develop.

Jump forward to the present day. As a sport we've now got many hundreds of top notch facilities around the world and routesetting is recognized as a big part of the success of any commercial facility. There have been tiny bits of information released over the years, but never a comprehensive manual for those looking to learn or improve on their existing setting skills. Around the turn of the century Scott Rennak and I kicked around the idea of writing a book (and Scott went on to produce a slimmed down pamphlet that saw very limited release). We both had visions of a complete volume: The Routesetting Bible. Not that either of us really considered ourselves the expert on the topic, but more because we both saw the need. Anyone that has spent any time setting will probably realize and agree that to write the actual definitive book

*Pat Bagley*

on the subject would be a huge undertaking and that the book would probably be released in multiple volumes. There are simply too many variables and subjective considerations to take into account. Even just a brief outlining of the possible chapters could possibly spiral off down any of a number of related tangents. Without a doubt, this has probably kept any number of talented setters from writing a similar volume.

In 2003 I became motivated to look at the project again. At that time though I had my sights set on a more general book. One that would touch on all the major topics, but leave a lot of room for individual interpretation and application. So much of good setting comes down to the individual doing it. Their creativity, their vision, and the ability to present things in a way that makes sense movement-wise. If defining the art of setting too precisely, my fear would be that creativity and individuality would be stifled. That is the last thing that I would want. I released my vision of the book in 2004, under the title, The Art of Coursesetting.

The book was the first comprehensive book available on routesetting and was well-received. It was sold world-wide and I received great feedback from setters everywhere. The feedback was hugely rewarding personally and I made the commitment to make myself a better setter and to always strive to provide climbers the best that I had to offer. It also propelled me to become even further involved in the indoor climbing industry. I stepped up my hold shaping efforts, built many more climbing walls and gyms, taught more clinics, and have since gone on to open my own bouldering facility.

That original book's print run is now all but sold. Coupling that dwindling inventory with the many advances that have occurred in the industry and the newer competition and setting standards in today's routesetting world, I chose to not re-print that book. Instead I have updated and re-written it where those changes made sense. Much of the original information is still here, but hopefully there are enough additions and updates to make it a beneficial improvement on the original volume. I have also decided to upgrade the production quality of the book. The better quality paper and binding will help the book take more abuse, and the full-color (and updated) images will hopefully keep setters' and climbers' psyche high.

I also chose to change the name of the book for this edition. I grew up in Southern California, and most of my setting experience at the time of writing the last book had taken place here. "Coursesetting" was always the term used locally to describe what we all did. When it came time to write the book, it never dawned on me that outside my little geographic bubble that "routesetting" was the more recognized term. And while I do consider what we do to be an art, I feel that the new title, Foundations of Routesetting, better describes what I consider this book to offer.

Finally, it should definitely be admitted that this book contains not only my own viewpoints, but a collective consensus of the opinions of all those I've had the opportunity to set with and talk to, those who've taken my coursesetting clinics (and taught me as much as I've taught them), and those who've tried to express and share their thoughts on setting in years past. I see this much less of my book, as the embodiment of routesetting wisdom to this point. With all of this said, I am proud to offer this latest edition.

- Louie Anderson

# INTRODUCTION

Routesetting is a very important part of commercial indoor climbing; perhaps the most important part. It's responsible for setting good quality climbs, which will encourage climbers to try their best; provide them with a certain degree of education and training; make them feel vital, strong and successful; and perhaps inspire people new to the sport to become regular participants. In the simplest of definitions, these climbs are the product that commercial climbing facilities are selling to potential customers. If that product is not good, no one will support that particular business and will look elsewhere. By extension, the very success of indoor climbing facilities relies largely on their routesetting programs.

On the other hand, if the climbs are well set and offer enough variety to allow for enjoyment and progress by climbers of different size and ability level, the product will be much more appealing and the question of whether or not these customers will commit to the cost of use and/or facility membership shifts away from the climbs themselves. When this happens the routesetters have done their job.

While some of the topics covered in this book apply specifically to commercial setting, the vast majority of the setting principles discussed apply to all routesetting endeavors; whether you are setting on your garage woody, a private wall, or the largest gym in the world. Routesetting is a universal activity, regardless of the venue.

Whatever your knowledge of setting practices, this book is meant to be a foundational reference manual to the activity. It's main goal is to provide an overview of the different aspects of routesetting. Perhaps it will teach you new techniques; perhaps it will only reinforce what you have learned and are already doing. Either way, the following chapters, exercises and appendices are designed to help standardize the activity and allow for the best possible results from routesetters committed to setting the best climbs that they possibly can. Do yourself and those that climb on your creations a favor and make that commitment.

Vince Schaefer

*Caroline Treadway*

# Before You Start

## Who Are You?

Perhaps the most important part of setting involves being honest with yourself as to what traits you have and how they will apply to your setting. What are your specific climbing strengths? What type(s) of holds are easiest for you to use? What angles and types of terrain do you excel on? For every one of these questions you should be willing to answer in the negative as well; which of these challenge you, and are you worst at? Being in touch with your own abilities will help you gauge better the true difficulty of the climbs you set. See Appendix A on page 191 for a survey that may help in defining your skill levels in different aspects of the setting game.

Every setter out there has his/her own setting style. This may be a signature move or sequence or as particular as a specific type of hold that you will routinely grab out of the pile to set with. This is perfectly acceptable as your style, coupled with the style of the other setters around you, is the key to variety on your wall or in your gym. However, a good setter will always challenge him/herself by trying to set outside their comfort zone; instead of always forcing climbers to conform to his/her own personal style. You should routinely attempt to further your own abilities by watching other setters and asking for feedback on your climbs from them and other wall users. Try to take to heart the comments you receive and implement those that seem to make sense. Setting is an art and while many setters have good instincts, all setters get better with time. Don't be too cocky about what you can already do. Rather focus on what you cannot and how you can learn and improve.

## WHY ARE YOU SETTING?

What is the specific goal of your setting? Are you setting for yourself and a group of training partners on a private wall? Are you setting for the public in a commercial climbing gym? Are you setting on a school or recreation center wall? All of these environments have specific needs and expectations of the climbs you set.

If you're setting on a private wall you would be wise to talk with the users and understand the skill levels of the users. What difficulty levels do they like to climb at? Do they need projects to work towards, and if so how much harder should these be? What types of holds do they prefer to climb on? What types of holds do they need to learn better, and are they looking to you and your climbs to teach them?

In a commercial gym setting you will more than likely be in a supervised environment where a Head Routesetter will be giving you specific assignments. This is perhaps the most particular setting environment in which to work. The style of climb that you are setting and the difficulty of climb expected of you are part of a larger style and difficulty disbursement within the facility. For this reason you will need to be somewhat more exact in the final product, and in making sure that it meets the demands of your assignment. Realize that you are part of a team. Instead of looking down or belittling the other setters, you'd be better to work together to share your knowledge and to accept and learn theirs. When the team is truly reciprocal in their constructive criticism and sharing of ideas, there is perhaps no better environment in which to expand your setting skills.

Schools and recreation centers often cater to a specific age group, most commonly children. Be especially aware that your climbs are not too advanced in difficulty or techniques for these often beginning level climbers. Special consideration will need to be made to the height dependency of the climbs to make sure that they do not exclude the smaller children.

*Caroline Treadway*

Whatever the facility in which you are setting, know your users and the specific demands that your climbs must meet. Happy users and management make for a positive setting environment. This is supposed to be fun. Do your part to make sure it stays that way - for all involved.

## What Makes a Climb Good?

Perhaps nothing is so difficult to define as a "good" climb. There are so many different factors involved and everyone seems to have different criteria for judging the value of a given climb. There are, however some basic considerations to keep in mind when planning your climb that will help it along the path to that sometimes elusive attribute.

**Who is it for?** As mentioned above. Every facility has a different user group. Knowing the abilities and expectations of this group will help you to better match all aspects of your climb to their needs. This should dictate every phase of your climb including the selection of the holds, the movement required to succeed on the climb, and the difficulty of the climbing itself.

**Is it friendly?** Most indoor climbers appreciate comfortable, user friendly holds, smooth transitions and nice consistent "flow" on their climbs. While not all outdoor climbing conforms to these criteria, most indoor climbing should. Tendon-threatening holds and painful body positions will not usually be appreciated or applauded by the masses. There will always be times that a specific singular climb might be acceptable with slightly more painful holds or a funky and awkward sequence, but these should be in the minority when looking at the total volume of climbs in the facility. Repetitive use of tweaky holds and execution of awkward movement can lead to injury, and should be avoided for the most part.

What does it teach? Indoor climbing was first pursued as a training endeavor, and many indoor climbers still see it as an exercise in improving their overall climbing abilities. In this context you can consider yourself the teacher. The climb that you set becomes the lesson. What does it offer in this regard? Many indoor climbs can be set to isolate and strengthen specific body parts, target weak techniques, force foot and hand precision, and reinforce good route finding skills by creating dead ends and irreversible moves as the penalty for poor choices, etc. There are no limits to what your climb could offer educationally to the end user. What instruction can and will you build into your climb?

**Is it Interesting?** When climbers are first starting out, basic left-right-left-right, "ladder" climbing is rewarding, but most climbers find this stale and unfulfilling after a short period of time. From that point on they look for challenge. Increased difficulty will always provide this challenge and as climbers progress, succeeding at harder climbs becomes the goal for some, but not all. The one thing that climbers of all levels will appreciate is creative movement. This is a very difficult thing to teach or even to learn. So much of it is instinctual and a combination of a setter's outside climbing experiences, his/her personal imagination and vision, and the ability to choreograph that into their setting. It's what sets apart great setters from the mainstream. Try to make your climb thought-provoking and interesting, but beware of making it too contrived or forced. Interesting movement is what will keep the climbers coming back for more. Do your best to deliver this most important aspect of indoor climbing.

## VISUALIZATION:

One of the first decisions you need to make when routesetting is where to set. Take the time to walk around the facility looking at all possible terrain options. Visualize different paths up the walls, and especially look for lines through the terrain that may be different from the normal line taken up that section of wall. Most gyms will have some sort of "signature" line that follows a prominent feature or section of wall. Perhaps a better adjective to use when describing a line like this would be "cliché." After a while the same old line will become stale (regardless of the difficulty or types of holds used) as the movement patterns become more and more repetitive to what have already been experienced. Challenge yourself to break from the normal formula used and change things up a bit. Another option is to set a variation to an existing climb. This is especially true when dealing with an existing climb that is traversing in nature. Often times it's possible to set a variation finish that branches off of the regular line part way up, or to set a variation or direct start that joins that climb at mid height. Not only do climbs like this increase the number of climbs available to wall users, but they eliminate what would often be wasted and unusable space on the wall. They also allow climbers to use moves that they have learned and mastered on the existing climb to benefit them toward success on your variation.

**Things to think about when visualizing your line include the following:**

- Where will the climb start?
- Where will the climb end?
- How can I incorporate the wall's features and angle changes into my climb?
- Where will the crux(es) be located?

For more thoughts on visualization, be sure to read Making the Most of the Terrain on page 30

## HOLD SELECTION:

Obviously one of the greatest factors in setting a popular climb is the type of movement that you include. The other main factor is the type of holds that you choose to set with. Due to the incredible variety of holds available and the infinite number of moves and combination of moves possible, there are no set rules or guidelines to refer to when choosing your holds. There are however, some considerations to keep in mind when doing so.

**Factors that should affect your hold selection:**

- How hard is the climb you plan to set?
- How steep is the wall you are setting on?
- How big, and how positive, are the other holds on your climb around the hold in question?
- How will the hold be oriented on the wall?
- Are there features, other holds, or wall panels near the hold placement that will affect its use?

Usually the size and how positive the hold is will somewhat dictate the difficulty of the climbing it generates, but not always. It's more correct to say that these hold traits, when coupled with the factors listed above and the corresponding footholds, will dictate the difficulty. Likewise, don't fall into the trap of setting easy climbs with big, positive holds and hard climbs with small, bad holds. This doesn't have to be the case in all instances.

You can make your easier climbs more interesting by throwing in the occasional bad or small hand or foot hold. As long as they are coupled with a larger hand or foot hold, or some other comfortable stance option (stems, heel or toe hooks, knee-bars, etc.), these holds can be just as usable as a larger or more positive hold option. In the same way, harder climbs can feature larger or more positive hand or foot holds as long as they are coupled with smaller or less positive hand or footholds, or an awkward and less-secure stance. Remember that the usability of a given hold is not just based on its size alone. It is a factor of three things: hold size, how positive it is, and what size the corresponding hand or foothold is. It's entirely possible for a small crimper with a decent foothold option and a huge sloper with the same foothold option to allow for the same difficulty of move. Also, a three-finger incut with a bad foothold option and a poor sloper with a huge foothold option may offer the same degree of usability. Don't be afraid to experiment and see what you can do to break away from your normal patterns.

As you are setting, you will also need to be aware of the size of the holds you are using and their placement in relation to other holds. The use of a larger, high-profile hold might make seeing foot holds located below it difficult. Similarly, placing a small hold above a larger hold may make it difficult to use or grasp in the way that you would like. While an absolutely static approach to the climb may eliminate these issues, don't count on all climbers being able to adopt the same level of control or smoothness that you anticipate or expect. As climbers tire or get on climbs above their level, they tend to rush and climb more dynamically. At times like this, these problems will manifest themselves to an even greater degree. Do your best to eliminate them altogether.

For more ideas on hold selection and their uses, see Holds on page 70

# SETTING SEQUENCE

There is no hard and fast rule regarding where to start when setting. Traditionally many setters start at the bottom of the climb and work towards the top and most people probably would say that this is the way it's done, but there is actually a lot of variety in setting sequence options.

**Ground Up** – As mentioned above, most people would guess that this is how it should be done. It seems logical, allowing the climb to unfold and develop in the order in which a climber will climb it and be exposed to its moves. This is in fact how the majority of climbs are set.

**Top Down** – An increasing number of setters are now starting at the top and working their way back down to the beginning. This is especially true when the crux or character section of the route is located at the top of the climb and the setter is concerned about transferring the moves to the wall as exactly as possible from the vision in his/her head.

**Crux First** – Similar to the concept of setting top down, many setters will set the crux of their climb first and then work outwards (up and down) from that sequence. This is especially true if the crux revolves around a specific hold, feature or wall panel and must fit into a limited space. As you might guess this setting sequence is most commonly used on harder, power-based climbs where the focus of the climb is on its crux.

**Hands First** – Sometimes referred to as "skeleton setting," this practice is often more efficient. It can be used with any of the above listed sequence options and is seen very frequently in different facilities. The thought process behind this type of setting is that it allows the setter to focus on hand movements without the distraction of trying to see the climb as a whole on the first pass of

*Photo by Natalia Boltukhova*

setting. Often handholds will be used as footholds once the climber moves past them and will eliminate the need for a foothold on that section of the climb. Setters that prefer this sequence will usually place all hand holds and then go back to the start and mentally (or actually) climb their creation adding footholds when and where needed.

You may need to vary slightly from this method if you have a move or sequence that revolves around the use of a specific foothold. For more info see Speed Setting on page 26

# EFFICIENCY

Setting takes time, bottom line. There are however, ways to make your setting time more efficient and productive. One of the most important exercises on the road to efficiency is planning. Before you begin, try to define as much about your climb as possible. This will allow you to make decisions and have answers to contingencies that might arise while setting before they occur. You will be able to act more instinctually while setting and flounder less when confronted with options. For more information related to planning see Before You Start on page 16 and Styles of Climbs on page 133

## The Ingredients:

A great way to make yourself more efficient as a setter is to be prepared. Take the time to select your holds before you start. This will not only help you to think ahead about what you intend to set, but will hopefully limit the number of times that you need to go back to the hold pile to look for a missing hold. When selecting your holds make sure that you also select some extras or alternates that will fit well with the other selected holds. Your hold need may change slightly as the climb becomes reality and you may be confronted with a situation where the original hold you selected will not fit in the space available on the wall or work as well with the other holds as you first thought it might. Likewise, gather together all necessary bolts (including a few extras in case you drop one), wrenches and other items that you might need during the course of your setting.

When setting roped routes where you will be off the ground for a length of time, it's a good idea to place all of these items into empty buckets, duffel or shoulder bags. These can either be clipped temporarily to your harness or clipped to anchors on the wall itself to take the weight off of your body. Having things close at hand will eliminate a lot of unnecessary up and down on your part as you set. You will invariably drop some needed item or forget something on the ground. For this reason it's nice to have enlisted the help of another setter, climber or gym employee on the ground that will be available to throw things up to you if needed. If you are going to be setting boulder problems or close to the ground, you can usually get away with just spreading things out on the ground around your work area. Not only does this make everything readily available, but it gives you the ability to scan your hold options quickly without having to dig through a bag or bucket.

## Speed Setting:

When faced with the need to set a lot of climbs, or when you have limited time in which to set a climb, it may be possible for you to benefit from one of the following methods:

**Skeleton Setting** – There are a few different thought processes here, given your preference and the environment in which you are setting. The basic premise behind skeleton setting is that the setter throws up an initial "draft" version of his/her climb with the intention of then coming back (immediately or later) and fine tuning or adding missing elements. This is especially useful when a setter is faced with a long day of competition or other setting assignments, where he/she wants to get their ideas onto the wall quickly without forgetting any of their other climb ideas. It also has value if a setter is trying to stake a claim to certain holds or sections of wall for his/her climbs.

The most common method of skeleton setting has the setter placing all required hand holds only on the first pass and then going back to add footholds. Another is to just throw up the cruxes of a series of climbs and then to return to finish the setting. Lastly is the lesser seen option of installing temporary markers (usually colored tape) on the wall to diagram out the path of a climb, prior to selecting and placing the holds. This is seen less and less as setters realize that hold selection and the way in which the holds relate to each other are as important as the movement itself. Regardless of the method chosen, the intent is to get a basic expression of the climb on the wall quickly and efficiently.

Regardless of which method you choose, when Skeleton Setting, the focus is getting ideas and holds on the wall (often many climbs), with the fore running and tweaking of the climb(s) coming later.

**Difficulty First** – If faced with setting many problems of ranging difficulties, it's generally best to start with the harder climbs and then set downwards in difficulty finishing with the easier climbs. When setting at or above your difficulty limit, the climbs will generally take longer for you to set and require a more concerted creative effort to make interesting. By setting these early in the session you can eliminate the mental stress often associated with their setting early rather than to deal with the demoralizing and draining effect that it can have when left till the end of the session.

In a similar way many setters will choose to begin by setting the most difficult section of their climb(s) and to then fill in the remainder of the moves around that crux. This is especially helpful when setting hard or power-based climbs.

## Positioning:

Depending on the length of your climb, your comfort level and the systems available, there are several different ways to get in location for setting. Regardless of the method you choose to employ, make sure that your safety system is bombproof. When clipping yourself into floor or wall anchors, always make sure that you have a back-up anchor in case your primary anchor fails. Many setters have preferences one way or the other and most options have their pros and cons. Here are some of the options:

**Ladders** - Some setters prefer setting off ladders (regardless of height) due to the fact that they can run up and down the ladder to get things as needed. The downside of this is that you will often have to run up and down the ladder. Setting off ladders also allows you to get exactly where you would like to be positioned. Again there is a downside here in that you will continually be moving the ladder to install different holds. Make sure that when setting off taller ladders that someone holds the base of the ladder if needed until you are in position and anchored.

**Aid** – When setting longer climbs on steep terrain, setters will often resort to the use of quasi-aid climbing techniques. The setter will anchor one end of a rope to either a ground anchor or another bomber anchor on the wall itself. He/she will then climb up to a given lead anchor (feeding out slack using a Gri-Gri or other auto locking belay device), clip their rope into the anchor and install the holds within reach of that anchor. They will then climb to the next anchor and repeat the process until they are finished installing the holds. Often times the existing lead anchors will be positioned too far apart from each other (or in the wrong location) to allow the setter to install the holds where they would like. In this instance the setter will usually place a bolt hanger into a t-nut anchor using a mounting bolt and clip into it temporarily to control their position on the wall. This works well and is common practice, but you should realize that hangers installed into t-nuts should not be considered strong enough to support the weight of a fall, should one occur.

**Toprope** – If the wall on which you are setting is not overly steep, you can set up a toprope over the line of your intended climb. If the wall is steep enough to warrant it, you may need to backclip the rope into some directional anchors (either existing lead anchors or setter placed hangers as described above). Once the toprope is positioned, the setter can alternately rappel down or Gri-Gri and jumar up the rope as required. Again usually one end of the rope will be securely anchored to simplify the necessary rope work.

**Man lifts** – Those that have had the luxury of setting using scissor of boom lifts should consider themselves lucky (and spoiled). Often only practical during the initial setting of new facilities or when setting on temporary walls, nothing is as nice or convenient as setting off a lift. You can position yourself directly where you would like to be and most lifts have a large enough working platform to allow for storage of all setting supplies and the safe testing of the moves while climbing only a few feet above a solid landing surface. There are some gyms out there that own their own lifts and use them regularly, but usually once the floor padding has been installed in a facility it is no longer practical to drive a lift around without either damaging the padding or reducing the safety of the lift itself.

*Justen Sjong*

# MAKING THE MOST OF THE TERRAIN

Different indoor climbing walls offer different types of terrain. There are the obvious differences of height and steepness, but they also have several different and distinct terrain qualities that set them apart. One may have a long blunt or sharp arete that has caught your eye. Another may have an extreme bulge or roof that seems the perfect spot to set your climb. Perhaps your wall has several angle transitions and smaller features that you want to incorporate into your climb. There's something to be said for an awkward or funky transition and the difficulty that it can add to a climb, but unless that's specifically what you're looking for, your goal when setting on anything other than a flat wall should be to make the angle transitions seem natural and flawlessly designed. The way in which you use these terrain traits goes along way toward insuring that your climb "flows" well.

If you are able to consistently set to accentuate and compliment the terrain of your wall, it will translate into considerably more realistic climbing and appreciative users. In a community of gyms where the setters have recognized the traits that their walls' terrain offer, switching from gym to gym can be like visiting a different crag. To a certain degree you'll have a different experience due to the fact that you'll be climbing on different setters' creations, but the characteristic that will lead the most to this feeling is whether or not the gym's setters are using their terrain well. Just as a specific outdoor crag can come to be known for a specific wall, feature or style of climbing; so too can your gym. If the setting style matches the terrain this is all the more noticeable and appreciable.

## Natural Features:

Many of climbing gym facilities have walls that contain an assortment of natural features. The use of these features on your climb will not only validate their inclusion in the wall's design, but can often lead to a more natural and organic feel to the climb itself. Once a wall has been climbed on for a period of time the regular wall users may tire of the feature and its perceived intrusion into the style of the climbs set around it. Because of this, challenge yourself to use the feature in ways that it is not normally used. Is it usually used as a hand hold? Try setting a little higher or off to the side from the feature and make it the key foothold for progressing past this section of the wall. Realize that in most cases if a natural feature is within reach (by hands or feet) to your climb that many climbers will attempt to use it. In this way you're usually much better off including it in your climb than marking it off and risking what may seem to be a contrived avoidance of it.

## Arêtes:

Home of the "barn door" move, where an unbalanced body will tend to hinge away from the arete like an opening barn door. The resistance against this type of move embodies the nature of arete climbing. Try to mimic this outdoor phenomenon by making at least some of your moves balancy. This can be achieved by placing the feet very close to arete itself and by not alternately placing all subsequent handholds on opposite sides of the arete. Having to make two or more hand movements on the same side of the arete will put the climber's body out of its natural cross-body alignment and force a lot more resistance into their movement. This is intensified if the handholds are faced toward the arete instead of away from it.

Remember when setting on arêtes that holds located around a corner, lip or arête often seem much more positive than when placed on the same plane as the climber. Because of this, you can often use much smaller or slopier holds than you might think. Likewise, use caution when selecting your footholds. Unless you intend for them to be used also as handholds, they will need to be very low-profile and bad. Using footholds such as these will not necessarily eliminate them as options for handholds, but will make them at most an intermediate or bumping hold. Smaller feet are also advisable in that they will not usually allow the climber to hook or pull in with his/her feet. Smearing footholds work well on arêtes as they will allow progress, but often will also push climbers in the direction of the barn door, requiring an increase in the amount of resistance that the climber needs to maintain in order to stay on the wall.

Arêtes often involve a lot of hooking (heels and toes) on the arete itself to maintain balance and to take the weight off of a given hand to allow for its movement. Because of this you may not always need a foothold for each and every hand movement. Play with the idea of hooking or smearing on the arete itself as you set your climb. You may be surprised at the movement you find as a result. Likewise, if the arete is not too rounded or subtle, you may be able to use the arete itself as a handhold along the line of your climb. Arêtes found outdoors often have long sections where there is no definable and specific handhold, but rather the climber is slapping his/her hand higher and higher up the arete in search of an eventual hold. Setting a section such as this on your climb will add a lot of realism to the line.

## Roofs and Bulges:

Perhaps more so than any other feature, roofs and bulges intimidate climbers. They provide the obvious focal point for difficulty on a specific climb. Whether you choose to place the crux of the climb on this terrain or not, this is where most will expect to find it. For no other reason than this, it's sometimes nice to position the most difficult moves after this feature. A climber will make it through the obstacle only to be confronted with a difficult series of moves when they thought they were home free. Other times you'll want to deliver respective of their expectations and position the business right in the midst of the steepness. The way in which you use holds on these sections of wall will directly impact the way in which a climber will move over or through it.

One of the easiest ways to control the ease with which a climber moves through the steepness is the way in which you face the handholds. If they face back towards the wall below the roof (underclings) the climber will generally be able to get good opposition with the footholds below and will be able to hang out and rest longer while considering the next move. An undercling will also allow the climber to statically reach closer to their maximum reach than one faced in a different direction. If the holds are positioned facing toward the intended path of travel away from the hold the climber will have to use considerably more body tension to keep his/her feet on the footholds. These handholds will also force shorter or more dynamic hand movements and reaches. These are the two absolutes of steep setting. There are obviously several other possible orientations for holds on steep terrain. Keep in mind that on ultra steep terrain climbers

*Caroline Treadway*

will always be on the lookout for footholds to give them the opposition necessary to use a given handhold. When these footholds are not perfectly placed, they will greatly increase the body tension required to climb the terrain, and the resulting difficulty of the movement. If the footholds are too far away, or non-existent, you will start to see more climbers losing their feet and/or committing to campus style movement. Roofs are the perfect terrain for the placement of knee-bars, toe hooks and bicycles (one foot pushing while the other pulls, often on the same hold).

## Slabs:

Often dismissed as "old school" or "beginner" climbing, slabs are probably the most under appreciated terrain in indoor climbing. No other type of terrain puts as much emphasis on footwork or allows for upward progress with as small of holds as does slab climbing. And while this does in fact allow for great learning terrain for beginners, it can also prove quite challenging for more seasoned climbers.

Many times, especially on textured and featured walls, you can eliminate the need for foot specific holds by merely forcing the climber to smear on the surface of the wall itself. How and where the climber chooses to place their feet greatly impacts their security and their ability to reach the next handhold. By not always setting specific footholds, or by forcing the climber to occasionally smear on the wall as an intermediate move, you are once again mimicking the real world and removing the security of seeing and knowing where the next foothold is located.

Slabs are also perhaps the best place to set mantle type moves. Depending on the angle of the slab, these can involve holds that are quite a bit smaller or less positive than you might think would normally be required. Play with the hold size and style a bit and you'll soon realize just how little it takes to accomplish this signature move. On less steep slabs you will usually be able to force the climbers to stand up on the mantle hold itself without the need for assistance from handholds placed higher. As the angle of the slab gets steeper you will either need to increase the size of the hold to allow for this or set some assistance holds within reach of the climber for use while they are making the mantle.

## Stemming Corners:

As with slabs, you can usually use much smaller and less positive holds in stemming corners. This is due to the fact that a climber will always have better opposition when climbing in a corner by placing hands and feet on opposite sides of the corner itself. Because of this direct opposition the climber will often be able to use the surface of the wall itself for foot purchase, and your requiring them to do so will force them to find the point of balance for their body size and the move at hand. You will also usually see a lot of hand-to-foot and a variety of mantle type moves in stemming corners.

The difficulty of the climbing is to a large degree dependent on how close to the corner you place the hand and foot holds. The closer into the corner they are placed, the more the climber will be pushed out of the corner. The farther away from the corner they are placed, the more secure the climber will be and the more he/she will be able to rest along the way.

In a way similar to, although directly opposite, arête climbing, putting two or more subsequent handholds on one side or the other of the corner will often make the climbing more difficult by removing the direct opposition between the two hands and by placing more dependence on the foot on the opposite wall from the hands. This is especially true when the handholds are directional and facing into the corner. If the handholds are directional and facing away from the corner this method of handhold placement will take the climber out of a stemming position and he/she will bring both feet onto the same wall as the handholds. By playing with a combination of these options you will be able to make the climber transition into and out of a stemming position and cause him/her to stay on whichever wall of the corner you so desire. If you have the luxury of a very long stemming corner in which to set you may want to increase the amount of climbing available to the climber by forcing several of these transitions along the length of the climb.

## Lips:

Usually found at the end of a roof or severe bulge, lips present one of the best options for heel hooking in indoor climbing. Whether it be to allow the security necessary for a key clip or to allow the climber to use a bad handhold, a hookable foothold placed off to one side or the other and just over the lip will give the climber a more comfortable and secure position than forcing them to try and keep there feet below on the steeper terrain.

Remember that as with arêtes and other outside corners, that holds located around lips do not need to be as large to accomplish the same thing. You will often see a large sloping hold placed at the lip of an overhang. When first grasped it will usually be more than positive to hold, but without the security afforded by a more positive hold if the climber loses his/her feet, causing the body to swing out beyond the plumb line from the handhold. When setting a heel hook move at a lip feature, the use of a less than secure handhold will force the climber to instinctually look for a hooking foothold. The placement of the heel hook will once again allow for a feeling of security when using the poor handhold, as it will take a lot of the climber's weight off of the handhold.

# USE OF FOOTHOLDS

Joe Iurato

The way in which you use footholds on your climbs can set the tone for the entire climb and go a long ways towards the way climbers regard your setting skills. When watching high level climbers, people often notice their footwork. The precision and complimentary way in which they place their feet is a learned skill. Climbing on indoor walls is a perfect place to practice and perfect that skill. As such, the burden is on you, the setter, to provide climbs that offer learning opportunities and present footwork options that the climber may or may not have yet been exposed to.

## What's On?

There are three basic choices when deciding the way in which footholds will be implemented into your climbs. These are All Feet, Marked Feet and Tracking.

**All Feet** – Often considered the lazy approach to setting. The climber can use any and all possible options for his/her feet for progress on the climb. In most cases this severely limits the creativity of the setter as the moves can generally be done any number of ways, based on the footholds used for the moves. This is the style of foothold use that is common when setting for children. It allows the setter to not concern him/herself with the possibility of creating height dependent moves that might otherwise prevent the child from making the move. Some facilities opt to allow children under a certain age to use all footholds when on climbs that may have been set for larger climbers initially. While this approach allows for little investment on the part of the setter or facility, it really does not provide anything of value to the climber in the sense of learning opportunities or development as a climber.

**Marked Feet** – The most common method of setting. In this type of setting any marked hold (whether intended for use by hands or feet) can be used by the climber for progress on the climb. This gives the setter the most options for creativity and to set specific foot sequences for the climber to follow. It also forces the climber to conform to the options presented by the setter and allows for the best learning environment for the climbers.

**Tracking** – No foot specific holds are set or are to be used by the climber. Instead all marked hand holds on the climb are to be used as possible footholds as well. There are times where tracking climbs feel natural (especially on steep roofs or caves), but they can often feel jerky when climbed on and they don't usually flow as well as those with specific supporting footholds set and marked. As mentioned when climbing on steeper terrain a section of tracking can provide interesting toe and heel hook options and can help to develop a distinct character to the climb or its crux section.

All of these options can be used exclusively or on only certain portions of your climb, and specific larger features or holds may be chosen to be off for your intended climb while others will be deemed usable. Likewise you may need an overly large foothold for a given move, but cannot think of a way to keep climbers from using it as a hand hold also. While every effort should be made to prevent this, in a worst case situation that foothold could be labeled "off" for hand usage. Just remember that if you are going to stray away from one of the three norms above that you will need to be precise in your markings and explanations of the climb's specifics.

## Foothold Size:

The size and how positive your footholds are will often go a long way towards determining how much weight will be placed on the climbers' arms and handholds. Smaller footholds and smears can be used on steeper walls to increase the amount of body tension required of the climber. Larger or more positive footholds can be used to provide opposition into directional hand holds and to take the weight off poor quality hand holds, making them more usable. Incut and higher profile footholds when used in roofs and caves can allow for toe and heel hooking options or drop knees that allow the climber to rest and/or enjoy a more comfortable stance. In many ways, the size of the footholds you choose to use will be every bit as important as the size of the hand holds.

When setting easier climbs you may want to keep the foothold size slightly larger. Beginning climbers often do not yet have the foot strength required to stand on smaller holds, nor do they yet trust their feet or give their footwork the attention it deserves. As you set harder climbs feel free to use smaller and often tiny footholds where their use makes sense. By doing this you are requiring the climber to focus on their footwork more and to be precise with their foot placement or risk failure. Often when using these smaller footholds, they are presented merely to help the climber maintain balance and proper body positioning. In this respect they act in supporting roles, where other footholds might provide the key to generating force or movement on a specific sequence of the climb.

## Foothold Positioning:

Where you choose to position the footholds in relation to the handholds will greatly affect the overall difficulty of your climb. Put them in the perfect position and the climber will enjoy comfortable stances and be given the necessary opposition to use holds that are oriented in other than horizontal positions. Place them away from where the climber would like them and he/she will be forced to struggle to use them and obtain a balanced stance.

If you are trying to force dynamic movement, place the footholds higher than normal. This will usually push the climber away from the wall and out of the comfort zone, requiring a less controlled and static movement style. In many cases these footholds will be the driving point and the main ingredient on generating the force required for the move a climber is faced with.

You can place the footholds high and off to the side to allow climbers a target hold to hook and pull themselves over to the next hold with. This is especially helpful on traversing or diagonal climbs or when transitioning from one wall panel to an opposite or adjacent panel.

When setting drop knees, stems, liebacks or other moves where the foothold is responsible for driving the climber's hand into the hand holds, your positioning of the footholds is all important. Likewise, the orientation of the hold is critical. To provide the most support possible for the climber, orient the foothold in direct opposition to the hand hold in question (the two holds should face into each other). The more you deviate from this pure positioning the harder it will be for the climber to gain the necessary support from the foothold and the more difficult the move will be.

Finally, adding additional footholds in key locations may eliminate the height dependency of a climb or individual move. Be aware of any additional help that the extra hold might offer to taller climbers and try to position it in such a way that it helps those that need it, but not those that don't. For more info see Height Dependency on page 40

## Cruxes:

Cruxes don't always need to revolve around a hand hold or series of them. Feel free to make the use of a specific foothold the focal point of your climb's crux. This crux can either revolve around a foothold that is in an awkward or less than ideal position for the move at hand, or one that is small, smeary or otherwise difficult to use in conjunction with the corresponding hand holds.

*Czar Goss*

# HEIGHT DEPENDENCY

This is often thought to mean that a move is too reachy, however height dependency can mean the opposite as well. Sometimes taller and longer-framed climbers will have difficulty fitting into particularly compact or scrunchy positions that fit smaller climbers just fine. Both definitions apply in regard to route setting and both should be avoided in most instances.

Occasionally you will find yourself having set a very interesting and creative sequence that gives an unfair advantage to one body size or another, with no real way to make the effort required equal for both sizes. This **may** be OK, as outdoor climbs sometimes favor one or the other without offering alternatives as well. As a setter though, you should do whatever possible to eliminate this from occurring. There is usually a way in which to avoid this altogether or to allow climbers of the opposite body size to still succeed on the sequence. Remember that, especially in commercial route setting, the goal is to make the climb's challenge of comparable difficulty for climbers of all sizes.

The easiest way to fix a height dependent move or sequence usually involves adding additional foothold options. The challenge when doing so is to try to prevent these extra footholds from making things easier for the other body size group, or offering intermediate hand holds. By placing the footholds in exaggerated positions relative to the original foot options (far to the side, extremely low or extremely high) they will be less likely to benefit the opposite climber group than the one you are trying to assist. In general terms, scrunchy moves can be made easier with wider or lower foot options and long or reachy moves can be made easier with higher feet. Often times the resulting move may be different or harder than the original and this is perfectly acceptable (within reason) as your main intent should be to make the move feasible for climbers of different sizes, not necessarily the same.

Be aware of the different body spans represented by the moves you are setting. There is more than one span distance that can create problems. Often times a climber of a differing body size will be able to reach the target hold, but because of the body span position will not be able to generate the movement necessary to actually use it. In fact just about every possible span can make a problem height dependent.

These include the following:

- Hand to hand span
- Foot to same side hand span
- Foot to opposite side hand span
- Foot to foot span

A good way to check your spans while setting is to use the arm test. To test this way, place your base foot (or hand) on the starting hold in question and reach toward the hand hold in question. If your fingers just reach the hold it will likely be too reachy for climbers much shorter than you. Specifics of this test will differ based on your size relative to the body size that you're checking against, but most setters aim for the target hold to be equal to their elbow or thereabouts. Shorter setters might use their mid-forearm, while taller setters might use their mid-bicep. The basic premise is the same regardless of your size. If a move honestly passes this test (and the concern is that the move might be too reachy) it should not be considered a height dependent move at all, but rather a power or strength dependent move.

*Any of these spans can make a move height dependent*

# FORCING A MOVE

There will be times that you would like to force an individual move or sequence of moves. Beware that when you are doing this you are setting yourself up for having climbers find a way around the intended move or sequence. This is especially true when you have a climb that incorporates traverses that then double back above themselves higher up. Today's climbers are getting more and more proficient at dynamic movement and you'd be surprised what some people will see as possible, and succeed at sticking. While you will probably not always be able to eliminate the option of someone cheating or skipping a move, it's nice to do whatever you can to make sure that this option is at least as hard, or harder, than the intended sequence. The basic rule of thumb when trying to force a given move or sequence is to make your way the easiest of all possible options.

There are several ways to force your intended move using certain types of holds as well as specific types and locations of footholds.

*Caroline Treadway*

## DYNAMIC MOVEMENT:

If you want to force a dynamic movement try placing the driving foothold for the move higher than what would normally be comfortable. This will usually push the climber's body away from the wall out of the comfortable and stable zone where core strength allows for more static movement. A very strong climber may still do the move somewhat statically, but will more than likely need to use a flag of some sort for stability and will probably end up doing a more difficult single move than your intended dynamic move. Using a higher driving foot will also enable you to place the target hold slightly further away making a static solution even more difficult to achieve.

## Specific Hand Usage:

If you are trying to force a climber to use a specific hold with a given hand you should first try to sequence your intended moves to where the most logical sequence would have the climber doing just that. Other than this you can make this particular hold a little tighter or more of a single-use hold that's difficult to match in. This will make a savvy climber realize the inability to match and they will make every effort to grasp it with the correct hand. By setting a long reach or lateral movement off this hold, away from the intended hand, you can also create somewhat of a "dead end" if the climber grasps the hold with the wrong hand. If this type of move is built into the middle or upper portion of the climb the climber will need to make sure that he/she is in correct sequence while approaching the hold or risk getting shut down when they reach this hold.

## Gastons versus Sidepulls:

Gastons and sidepulls are among the best types of holds to use to keep a climber where you want them. First you must realize the body positioning used with each of them. Imagine a given hold on a climb. Almost without exception if this hold is a gaston the most comfortable and stable position in which to use it puts the climber close to the hold, with the hold itself near the climber's grasping shoulder. On the other hand a sidepull used in the same location positions the climber further away from the hold, where the most comfortable and efficient body position is often found with the arm at or near full extension. If you are trying to keep a climber away from or closer to a given hold, feature or other obstacle, the use of one or the other of these hold types is often the answer. The proper placement of a supplemental foothold (usually allowing for good opposition with the grasping hand) of sufficient size will often magnify whatever positioning properties the hold might offer.

## Which Hand Moves?

If you want to push a climber to leave a given hold (or pair of holds) with a specific hand, make the hand to remain more positive than the one you would like to see move. It goes against human nature to feel good about leaving a position of comfort and control for one that is less secure. In this way the odds are greater that the climber will go with the hand that you intend. You can do more to ensure this by giving the climber a well-placed foothold that supports and/or gives opposition to the hand that you would like to see remain, or offer a higher foothold option that becomes the driving foothold for your intended move. In general terms whichever side this higher, driving foot is on - that will be the hand most likely to move.

## Should it be Changed?

Finally if your efforts have proven unsuccessful and climbers have found a way around your intended sequence, ask yourself if it really needs to be changed. Often times outdoor climbs have multiple sequences possible to conquer a certain portion of the climb. In some ways this can be a compliment to your setting (especially if the alternate sequence favors a climber size that was excluded from your original sequence). As long as the difficulties are comparable, there's probably nothing wrong with having the climber succeed using different techniques or sequences.

It also should be noted that having climbers find a different sequence than you intended can be seen as an opportunity to evaluate your setting and learn from the experience. What could you have done differently to avoid having this happen? What did the climbers do that you did not see as an option? Could you have used different holds for the moves that would have reinforced your intended sequence and lessened the likelihood of other sequences? Remember that while we are the architects of the climbers' movement on our climbs, we should not be dictators of movement or let our ego cloud our setting. If someone finds another option or sequence, simply accept it and try to learn what you can from the experience. Once the initial fore running process has been completed, you generally should not continue to tweak a climb to force your intentions on the climbers. To do so is unfair to those now attempting to succeed on the climb.

Jennifer Gold

# ROUTE SETTING FOR CHILDREN

Artificial walls are becoming more and more popular with children. Whether it's in the form of a visit to the local rock gym for a birthday party or as an everyday gym user, we're seeing more and more kids climbing the walls these days. With this influx of younger, smaller climbers comes the need to be able to route set with their size and limitations in mind. While not everything in the gym need necessarily be set to these standards, a setter must be able to provide options for the kids and have them be realistically rated, based on their abilities and size.

The most obvious consideration when setting for kids is reach. This would better be defined as span, because the distance from foot to hand is not the only concern. The spans from foot to foot, hand to hand and across the body (opposite hand to opposite foot) need to also be taken into consideration when setting for kids. Any one of these can make the move too "reachy" for a given child. When setting kid-specific climbs don't be tempted to just add a bunch of extra feet. Instead, try to scale down the entire climb to fit a child-sized body. As kids develop as climbers they will need to have creative climbs on which to train as well as any adult would. Setting climbs where they continually jump from hold to hold, and where they need to match (hands, feet or feet to hands) on everything does little to develop them as climbers.

When testing the reachiness of your climb it's best to develop a point of reference on your own body to equate to a certain size of climber. This is similar to the technique used when making sure that your climbs are good for shorter climbers (see Height Dependency on page ???), but instead of using your elbow as the point of reference you may need to use the middle of your bicep, or even your shoulder. Once you have set a handful of climbs using this technique, watch a few kids climb them and adjust your point of reference accordingly. Once established, you will be able to incorporate this into your setting very easily and quickly.

Another consideration when setting for children is to be careful of the radius of the holds you set with. Kids have much smaller hands than adults and as such larger slopers, pinches and other holds with a wide radius will be far less positive for children than for adults. Conversely, many holds will be more positive due to children's smaller finger size. What might be a one-pad incut or 2-finger pocket for an adult will be quite a bit larger for a smaller hand, and might feel more like a two-pad incut or a 3 or 4-finger pocket. Using any of the monster-sized roof jugs on a kid's climb is probably not required when looking to achieve the same effect that they would have on an adult climb. A normal large or extra-large jug will do the same thing and would more than likely be even more positive due to its more compact hand sizing.

Lastly, unless you are setting for more experienced child climbers, be aware of the moves that you are setting. A beginning child climber will not likely understand more complex movements and techniques. Climbs set to include them may seem considerably harder due to this lack of vision and understanding. This is not to say that everything should be set left-right, left-right, etc., but that it should be fairly straightforward and easier to figure out. For the most part, it's important to encourage beginning child climbers and allow them to enjoy the activity. Too much frustration early on will only cause the child to sour on the activity and likely they'll lose interest and quit climbing altogether.

Be careful also of setting overly stressful moves as well if children climbers are the focus of your climb; especially on more difficult climbs. Movements that are intensely stressful on shoulders, fingers, etc. may be more than what a child's body has been conditioned to deal with at this point in their climbing career. Don't necessarily avoid these movements; just keep any possible physical risks in mind relative to a younger climber's bodily development.

As children improve in their abilities make sure that you set more difficult and thought provoking climbs for them to challenge themselves on. Be sure to always remember the considerations mentioned above, but don't insult the children's abilities by continuing to set juggy ladders for them. Many of today's best climbers are young and you may just be setting for a future World Cup champion.

*Dan Brayack*

# SETTING OUTSIDE YOUR RANGE

There are going to be times when you'll be expected to set climbs outside your range. This can have a few different meanings. The most obvious is setting climbs that are more difficult than you can personally climb. Other meanings would include setting using types of holds that you are not proficient at using or setting on angles that you aren't comfortable climbing on. Realize that you are not alone and that all setters have to deal with this at one time or another. Whether you are setting a climb for gym users based on an assignment from your head route setter, setting for a competition, or setting a project for yourself and your friends, there are many ways that you can make your task easier and the end result more accurate and enjoyable.

One of the most important elements when attempting to set outside your range is honesty. First and foremost you need to be honest with yourself when it comes to your abilities. Not only as they relate to strengths, but equally as they relate to weaknesses. If you have a regular climbing partner ask for their input when assessing your abilities. For a quick survey that might help to this end see Appendix A on page 191. This assessment of your abilities is key when setting outside your range as you will use it as a starting point to move away from in gauging the difficulty of your setting project.

# Angles:

If you're faced with setting on an angle that you aren't comfortable climbing on, try to see the project as an adjustment of a similar climb on your favorite angle. When first getting used to setting on a new angle it's generally easier and more efficient to set the climb as you would on an angle in your comfort range, but to adjust the hold size accordingly. If it's steeper than you're used to the holds will need to be proportionally bigger. If it's less steep they can be smaller. Each angle of steepness brings its own techniques and styles of movement to the game, but initially it all comes down to hold size. Your education and awareness of the finer points will come in time. The most important base component is making sure that the hold size is appropriate for the difficulty and angle of the climbing.

Think also about the incut nature of your chosen hand holds. A hold that is flat and usable on a lesser angle will become slopey on a steeper angle. The same thing holds true for jugs. A rounded incut may be very juggy feeling on a 20 degree overhang, but when placed on a 45 degree overhang may feel far more slopey and less secure. On ultra-steep angles, jugs that have a double incut will allow the security of a single incut shape on lesser angles. Using a normal jug on roofs and angles much greater than 45 degrees overhung will likely require the use of large, supporting footholds, and using them will need to be a consideration. Adjusting the size and placement of these supporting footholds will drastically affect the difficulty of your climb.

Keep in mind also that the size and positive nature of footholds become very important as the angle of climbing changes. As walls become steeper the footholds will generally need to become more positive to accomplish the same thing. On ultra steep angles the footholds will need to be incut and positive enough to hook for some types of moves. If you're trying to force more dynamic movement on these steep angles a flat or slopey foothold that has a higher profile will give the climber enough contact area and purchase to generate movement, but not to stabilize or hook. As walls get less steep the footholds can be much smaller or non-existent, forcing the climber to use the wall surface itself for smearing as an intermediate move to gain the next hold.

# Hold Type:

So you're good on pockets, but now you're faced with setting a climb using primarily slopers. What could be more different? Rather than be hesitant and apprehensive when attempting to set with a different hold type, you'd be better off looking for similarities and working from them as a base. Climbing, and even more so indoor climbing, is based on movement between a set of hold options. The basic movement has similarities and patterns than transcend hold type. Of course you will need to make small adjustments and considerations when using a different type of hold, but perhaps not as much as you think.

There is definitely going to be a learning curve when absorbing the intricacies of different types of holds, but don't let that scare you away from experimenting. The best method of learning is to set a climb as you would with the type of holds you're used to, but substitute the new hold type and then climb it. You will learn as much by throwing yourself at the holds without the expertise of that hold type as you will any other way. As your weaknesses are magnified try to realize what about the move makes it hard for you and how it would be easier. Using these realizations as a base you will begin to understand better the nature of that style of climbing.

You'd also be wise to watch other climbers who excel on the hold type in question. How are they moving on the holds? What specific techniques do you see them using? What types of moves seem to give them difficulty or seem comfortable and easy for them? By being a good observer and then taking these observations and transferring them into your setting you may discover new styles and techniques specific to that hold type. You'll also learn a lot by speaking with other setters that may be more comfortable with this hold type than you are. When setting never be afraid to ask for others' help or input on your setting. While the feedback that you obtain may not always seem appropriate or what you were looking for, you may just get that kernel of wisdom that makes it all "click."

## Difficulty:

Often the most challenging range to set outside of is your difficulty range. While most setters would agree that it's difficult to set climbs much harder than what you can personally climb, few acknowledge and adjust their setting style when setting climbs far below their personal climbing level. Both setting extremes should be approached with caution, and your setting styles will need to be adjusting accordingly in either case.

**Setting Easier** – Setters will seldom put the same effort or creativity into setting climbs well below their abilities. This is wrong. You must realize that you are performing a service and that service, while initially for the benefit of your employer, is ultimately being performed for the end user – the person who attempts your climb. If you're going to take the time to set a climb, take the time to give that climb the full benefit of your setting skills. More so than experienced climbers, the climbers who will be attempting these easier climbs are in need of creative, well set and educational climbs that will help them to take their climbing to the next level. It's your job to provide this.

One of the most common mistakes made when setting for lower level climbers is to not adjust the holds and movement to match their abilities. Stronger and more experienced climbers have better technique, stronger fingers, better open hand strength and more confidence when faced with a difficult move or sequence. Expecting these same levels of experience and skill from lower level climbers when setting for them will result in climbs that are too difficult, challenging or require a higher level of commitment than climbers at that level might be able to achieve. Likewise if you build certain moves or techniques into your climb that those climbers may not yet have been exposed to or learned they will not see it as an option and will either fail or be forced to commit to a much harder move than what you intended. Setters need to do everything possible to match the type and size of holds, and the style of movement to the level at which they are setting.

**Setting Harder** – When attempting to set climbs that are beyond your own climbing level don't be discouraged or apprehensive. All setters have had to do this at one time or another and if nothing else it's a great way to test your setting limits and to perhaps learn something new.

Ultimately you will be guessing at the grade. What you should attempt to do is to approach the climb logically and make your guess as educated as possible.

Don't assume the holds have to be bad to make a climb hard. The easiest way to initially begin setting climbs past your limit is to imagine that you are setting a climb at your limit instead. However, when selecting the holds for your climb pick the same type of hold that would you normally use and make them slightly smaller or a little less positive (and do the same with the footholds). This alone will ensure that the climb is harder. Usually the crux on most indoor climbs is just a few grades harder than the rest of the moves, so you can also simply set a climb with the majority of the moves being about 2-3 grades below your target grade. Then step up the difficulty a notch or two for the crux and you'll be pretty close to your goal.

If there are other climbs set that are of similar difficulty to your target grade you can also compare the intensity of the moves on the existing climb(s) to those that you are setting. Have other setters or climbers that climb closer to the level of your climb try the individual moves, as it's easy to set too difficult of moves when first attempting to set above your limit. You should also make sure that you are not missing alternate sequence options that might be easier than your intended sequence. Higher level climbers often have mastered different techniques and can see options that you may not have yet been exposed to. Having these other climbers try the moves will also alert you to the possibility of this.

Finally, be honest with yourself regarding your strengths and weaknesses. Ask yourself why you cannot do the climb. If it's just a lack of flexibility, body tension, finger strength, etc. and that area is one of your weak points, it's highly likely that a slightly better climber will be able to succeed on the climb. Conversely, if the style of the climb matches your strengths and you still cannot succeed on the climb it may actually be too difficult for those that do not share your strengths (even if they climb at a higher grade overall). There's a fine line sometimes when setting outside your range and it's very easy to cross it. The more you put yourself in this setting position, the more you will become aware and comfortable with what the moves should feel like, even if you can't do them.

# MARKING CLIMBS

The methods used for marking climbs are becoming more and more consistent from gym to gym. There are really only a couple of options in use. These are setting by color, using tape and using tags.

## Setting by Color:

This is pretty self-explanatory. A given route or boulder problem is set using hand and footholds of the same color. Once set, climbers will know that anything within reach of the same color is intended to be used (if needed) for the climb that they are on. This method offers the cleanest visual presentation to facility users.

Special consideration needs to be made that climbs set with the same color are not set closely enough to each other that they might present alternate options or sequences, that were not intended, by using the holds of the adjacent climb. Another thing to be careful of is setting climbs next to each other using colors that are not contrasting enough as to be discernibly different to most climbers. Sometimes gyms that are trying to maximize their wall space will resort to using colors other than the normal, more primary colors, causing confusion. Some examples of this would be a dark orange climb set next to a red climb, adjacent climbs where the green and blue holds have a similar hue, climbs where there are several different shades of the same color used, etc. Less common, but still of concern are climbers who have color blindness or difficulty with certain colors placed next to each other. It's difficult to cater to all clients with special needs, but if you know of a regular wall user with problems such as these take the time to ask the nature of their limitations and do what you can to avoid confusing situations for them. Even if you are unable to prevent the problem entirely they will appreciate the effort. One way that gyms are trying to avoid these confusions is by painting their holds (see Holds on page 70).

*Start and Finish Tape Options*

## Setting Using Tape or Tags:

This is probably the method most commonly used to mark climbs on artificial walls. The basic premise is that all hand and footholds will be marked with a piece of colored tape (see Tools on page 92, for tape options) or patterned tag. Once set, climbers will know that anything within reach with the same marking is intended to be used (if needed) for the climb that they are on.

The same considerations need to be made when marking with tape or tags as when using colored holds (see section above) to avoid confusion or alternate climbing options. When marking the holds make sure that the tape or tag is placed in a location that will both be visible to the climber at the point when the hold is to be used, **and** a location where the tape or tag will not interfere with use of the hold or be damaged or removed by hand and foot traffic. In some instances a hold is used more than once while at different points on the climb and more than one piece of tape or multiple tags will need to be used. Most gyms prefer also that the tape or tag extend below the edge of the hold (and be sandwiched between the hold and the wall surface) so that if the tape stops sticking to the wall for whatever reason it will not fall off, but remain as a "flag" to mark the hold. Routine wall maintenance should be done to replace damaged or missing tape or tag markers, and all wall users should be encouraged to notify coursesetters or other staff members if they find a piece of tape or tag that is missing or needs to be replaced.

Many gyms prefer to install their tape or tags in the same orientation and with consistently sizes pieces of tape or tags. One example of this is to have all markers installed coming down from the right side of the hold at about a 45 degree angle. Facilities that standardize their marker orientation and sizing offer a much cleaner visual presentation than those that allow for random positioning and sizing. However, if all tape is installed in this manner, it can sometimes be difficult to see from above if the climber is moving in the opposite direction away from the hold.

There are a few simple patterns used to designate starting and finishing holds on a climb marked using tape or tags. The starting hold(s) will either be marked with a tape "V" , an inverted "V" or a tape box (picture on page 53). The finishing hold(s) will usually be marked in a similar manner. The style of marking is not that critical as long as it is consistent throughout the gym so that climbers are not confused. In the case of a bouldering wall, the problems will often finish

*Tape Pattern Options*

anywhere along the top of the wall. In this case a finishing hold or finishing box (see picture ?? below) will only be necessary if there is an exact intended finishing section or finishing hold. Try to avoid marking finishing boxes in bouldering areas unless they are really needed as this practice uses unnecessary marking materials, generates more maintenance work for routesetters and can lead to a very cluttered looking bouldering area.

If your have limited tape colors available and are forced to set overlapping or adjacent climbs using the same color of tape, patterns can be added to the tape using a permanent marker. These patterns should be limited to the three most widely used (and distinguishable) patterns. These are X's, stripes and dots (left page). Occasionally gyms will opt to use additional symbols (stars, smiley faces, peace symbols, short words, etc), but in most cases the use of too many symbols gets confusing and overwhelming when trying to spot holds while climbing. Another option is to stack a thinner tape stripe directly over a wider base length of tape. When creating striped tape markings like this, it's generally best to use tape colors that offer a sharp contrast to each other (i.e. red and white, black and white, yellow and blue, etc.) to make them more easily distinguishable from other markings.

The two most common type of tape used are duct tape and gaffer's tape. Different setters prefer one over the other, but both work well if a good quality tape product is purchased. The main difference between the two is that the duct tape is a vinyl tape and the gaffer's tape is a cloth tape. In some cases, the gaffer's tape will last longer and stick better, but it really comes down to personal preference in the end. Both are available in many colors and patterns. The duct tape generally comes in either 1 or 2 inch wide strips and the gaffer's tape is usually sold in one inch widths. When installing tape, you can greatly increase its adhesion by brushing along the length of the tape with a stiff nylon or brass wire brush.

## Climb Identification:

It's important to clearly identify different climbs in your gym. This serves several purposes, but is mainly used to inform wall users. Climbs are usually identified with a large piece of tape or information card attached to, or installed adjacent to, the starting hold(s) of the climb. It should always be placed on the highest intended starting hold. This way climbers will know automatically where to begin climbing (this is even more important when setting by color, where no other markers will be used). A good identification marker will present several pieces of information and will present all information in large, clear letters that are easily legible.

This information should include the name of the climb (if climbs are named in your gym), the rating of the climb, the color of holds or markers for the climb (if using tape or tags with patterns it's best to place an example on the tag for clarification), the date set, the date to be removed (if your gym uses an expiration program) and the setter's initials. In a competition setting the climb's competition number and the total point value for the climb should also be shown, and the rating, date and setter information is usually not included.

Other variations that can be used are tags of a different color (or a supplemental tag of some sort) to help climbers identify newly set climbs, and a consensus sheet. The first should be pretty self-explanatory, but if a supplemental tag is to be used make sure that it is large enough and recognizable enough that a climber doing a quick scan of the gym will notice it without having to resort to a closer, tag-by-tag inspection. The consensus sheet is something that many gyms are starting to use in order to diffuse rating arguments. In its simplest form; newly set climbs will only have a suggested rating (or rating range) shown on their information tags. On a separate portion of the tag (or on a supplemental sheet of paper) there should be an area for climbers to add their suggested rating after doing the climb. Once a given number of suggestions have been given (5-10 usually) the suggestions are averaged out and a final difficulty rating is given.

Other information that should be placed on the identification tag is any special rules or clarifications concerning the climb. These could include several possible things such as:

**Arete (or other feature) On (or off) route** – means that the named feature can or cannot be used on the climb. To avoid confusion features should all be "on" or "off" on most climbs.

**No Stemming** – similar to above and pretty self-explanatory.

**Any Feet** – means that footholds of any color or marking can be used on the climb.

**Jibs On** – means that jibs (see Holds on page 70) can be used for feet (or hands – clarify as such) on the climb, as well as any marked holds.

*Alexis Diller*

Clarification information regarding any variation finishes or link-ups to other climbs.

**Match Start or Jump Start** – means that the climb begins matched on a single hold or that the climber needs to jump to the starting hold(s).

**Sit Start or Standing Start** – defines the body position from which the climb begins.

**Tracking Only** – Only marked hand holds can be used for footholds.

**Finishes On ???** – Defines the finishing hold or section of wall where the climb finishes.

# FORERUNNING

Forerunning is a very important part of the routesetting process. Its importance is even greater in a competition setting environment and most setters are used to dealing with it there, however it's still valid for day to day setting. Forerunning is quite simply the checking of a newly set climb (usually by a group or someone other than the climb's setter) to make sure that it is all that it can be. The goal of forerunning is not necessarily to "fix" the climb. While it's true that the forerunner is looking to make sure that certain criteria exist according to the intended purpose of the climb, the forerunner should be careful not to eliminate whatever creativity and uniqueness the climb might possess. Every setter brings a different flavor to their creations. This is an important part of the setter's job and goes a long way towards achieving the diversity that most facilities strive for. The last thing the forerunner should end up doing is creating a whole gym full of homogeneous offerings that climb like his/her own creations. If this were the intent there would be no reason to employ the other setters at all.

The main things that the forerunner should look for are the following:

Is the climb of the correct difficulty?

Almost without exception a setter will create a climb based on a distinct need and with an assignment in mind. Because of this, it's important that the difficulty be accurate to what was expected. If the climb is of the correct difficulty there is nothing further to do in this area. If it's slightly too difficult or too easy changes should be suggested to allow for a final difficulty equal to that needed. If only minor grade adjustments need to be made this can usually be achieved by either changing out key holds and making them slightly larger or smaller, or by simply rotating one or more holds will achieve the desired result as well.

Changing foothold location may be an option as well. If you need to make the climb more difficult move some of the footholds to where they are in usable positions that are not quite as optimum for the attached movement. If you are looking to lighten things up a bit position the footholds in the ideal location and orientation for maximum assistance on a given move.

If the completed climb is considerably too easy or too hard perhaps it's best to leave it alone to fill a need for a climb at its current grade (especially if it's fun and involves creative movement as is). Sometimes it's more work to drastically change a climb's grade than it would be to start over, as once you begin changing one move it continues to affect the adjacent moves to the point that you are resetting the entire climb anyhow.

Is the climb reasonably attainable (at the same grade) for different sized climbers?

Primarily this becomes a check for height dependency (see Height Dependency on page 40). There will occasionally be some climbs that will favor a specific height or style of climber, but for the most part all climbs should be attainable by climbers of that skill level, regardless of size. Suggesting hold changes or additions will usually allow the problem to be remedied.

*Tim Kemple*

This assessment should not be limited to height dependency however. The forerunner should also be looking to make sure that the holds selected are usable regardless of hand size and that they are appropriate for the difficulty of the climbing and the angle of the wall(s).

Does the climb have an enjoyable and natural flow?

As mentioned above, the base creativity and style of a climb should be the work of the original routesetter. That said, if there is a single move or short sequence that seems out of place with the remainder of the climb, or if there is a transition that seems awkward or overly contrived, the forerunner should be prepared to point it out and if possible make suggestions on how to improve that section.

Are there any dangerous or unnecessarily painful holds used on the climb?

From time to time there will be a climb that has a theme or is designed to replicate a particular outdoor climbing style. Sometimes these will require the use of smaller crimps or incuts that "bite," or otherwise painful or awkward holds. In extremely limited quantities these climbs might be OK to leave as they are. In most cases, however the forerunner will be responsible to point out any painful holds or those that may be trapping (i.e.: holds that are extremely tight or are difficult to easily remove the fingers from when moving to the next hold). In most cases a replacement hold can be found that will still allow for the same type of movement, but will also provide for more comfortable use.

## Is the Climb Marked Adequately?

Upon first casual viewing of the climb, are all of the hand and footholds obviously marked? Are there any questions as to whether or not a particular hold, feature or adjacent wall panel can be used? Once the forerunner is actually on the climb, can he/she see all of these same markings and understand their meaning? If not, it's up to the forerunner to point out where additional markings could be installed, or where and how existing markings may not be adequate.

## Setting Experience:

Routesetting is a very complex activity. While in some cases (checking height dependency and rating) it will be OK to ask climbers of the size or ability level in question to try a climb, they often will be unable to make accurate suggestions for modification unless they have at least a rudimentary understanding of routesetting. While climb testers like these give a good representation of how a given move will be read by other climbers, in most cases forerunners should be experienced setters.

A forerunner with setting experience will be much better suited to offer suggestions and options (often several) as to how to achieve the desired effect of a move, sequence or climb. They will often be able to intuitively read the setter's intentions and with this in mind will be able to tailor their comments and suggestions to the same approach or climbing style. Every setter has their own skills and strengths and forerunners with setting experience may bring a whole new approach to the challenge at hand.

## Fitness:

A good forerunner should have the appropriate fitness level and climbing ability for the climbs that he/she is getting on. While most forerunners can usually offer valid input on climbs just below or above their own levels, the further they get away from their comfort zone – the more guesswork and speculation will become a part of their assessment. Forerunners need to be able to imagine themselves as the intended end user. Whether for everyday use or for competitions, the climbs being reviewed will need to be attainable and accurately rated for climbers at that level.

Pat Bagley

When forerunning climbs set for a competition, the forerunner should be aware of the format of the competition and should factor that into his/her approach to the climb(s). If it's an onsight competition, the forerunner should treat it as such and receive no beta prior to or during the first attempt. If there is a time limit or pattern that the competitor will be subjected to, the forerunner should match that limit or pattern during his/her review of the climb(s). The more consistent the forerunner's experience is with that of the competitor, the more specific the forerunner's input will be.

## Respect:

The routesetters do the brunt of the work when it comes to creating climbs. Whether the climb ends up being popular or a dud, the setter will be the one that receives the accolades or the insults. The forerunner will usually not even be acknowledged by the end user. Being aware of this and respectful of the setter's initial creation will go along ways towards insuring that the foreruner's comments are taken in the context in which they were intended. There are often big egos involved when dealing with setters and their creations, and the last thing a forerunner should want to do is to crush or challenge this creative energy. All comments should be made as constructively as possible. Likewise, if a forerunner is able to offer multiple solutions to a given challenge and leave it to the setter to make the final decision as to how to proceed, mutual respect can be maintained and the setter will usually still feel that the climb is his/her own creation.

## Honesty:

Not only will the forerunner need to be honest in the appraisal of a climb and its need for change, but also with the strengths and weaknesses that are part of his/her own climbing. These attributes will need to be considered when assessing a climb and a valid review of the climb will include adjustments as needed to compensate for them. If the forerunner is having a particularly good or bad day, this will have to be identified and accepted as part of the equation in order to

Mike Halsall

prevent climbs from being rated too easily or too difficult. Often the setters will be familiar with the abilities of the forerunner and whether or not the forerunner incorporates them into his/her judgement, the setter will.

*Caroline Treadway*

# HEAD SETTER DUTIES

This section is really intended for the Head Routesetter's direction only, and pertains to the management of routesetting staff. You are perhaps the most important member of the gym staff. The ultimate responsibility for the quality and quantity of the product that the gym offers to its users is in your hands. Because of this, you need to approach your job with professionalism and a serious commitment to the end result of your efforts and those of the setters under you. At the same time a certain amount of humility needs to be a part of your approach to dealing with the other routeesetters. You may not necessarily be the best setter in the gym, or the one with the most time spent turning a wrench. You may have been chosen because of your ability to be diplomatic and manage the setting team best. Don't let the position (and its power) go to your head. At the end of the day, you're just another routesetter to most people.

Historically, few gyms have operated a truly organized setting program. Most modern facilities have a better understanding and appreciation for the role of routesetters and place the requisite importance on hiring a skilled setting team. These gyms enjoy reputations for providing the best climbs around, and tend to have a higher number of climbers visiting their facilities. This is the type of return that gym owners need to see to warrant the hiring of additional setters, raising wages for setters and the purchasing of additional holds with which to set; all of which are probably on your wish list as the Head Routesetter. By implementing and maintaining some of the following programs, you can take the steps to make your setting program the best that it can be, and something in which you can take great pride.

## Setting Assignments

Know your setters. Know what they are capable of, and more importantly what they are not capable of. This knowledge will make issuing assignments to your staff much easier and allow for the best possible results. You should keep some sort of file on your setters. Many Head Routesetters keep this info in their head, but it's a much better idea to keep actual hard copy files. Information included in these files should certainly include their range of setting abilities, not just limited to difficulty levels, but also setting styles and angles that they are good or bad at (see page 191 for a sample questionnaire). Be honest with your assessments and update the file as things change (for the better or worse). You can also use this file to keep track of extra efforts made by the setter, competitions they were involved with (and in what capacity they served), and any important feedback (again good or bad) that you have received from other staff members and/or climbers regarding this setter's abilities and climbs.

When making assignments make sure that you allow setters to set what they like. Everyone will need to set below (or above) the level they would like to, or in areas of the gym that they do not frequent. If you also allow them options for setting what and where you know they would prefer they will be less likely to complain when given what they would otherwise consider a bad assignment. Also try to acknowledge potential in your setters. If you notice that a setter has skills in an area, allow that setter the opportunity to work with other setters that perhaps need help in this area. Conversely, if you see that a setter is lacking, try to team that person up with someone who excels in that area.

## Perks

Different gyms have set up their routesetting programs differently. One option used by many facilities uses setters that are trade members who are given a free membership to the facility for a given amount of time spent setting. If your facility is set up using a trade member arrangement try to implement additional perks to motivate your setters and get the most productivity from them.

The options for rewards can be anything from cash to day passes for the setter's friends to use, and anything else that you can imagine and would be seen as motivational and valuable to a specific setter. Perks are usually awarded based on fulfilling their assignments prior to a certain date, putting in extra hours or setting extra climbs, organizing or cleaning holds, forerunning and any of the other miscellaneous jobs required in related areas. When set up well, very basic perk offerings will guarantee that you not only get the most out of your routesetting team, but also that the morale and energy levels will be kept high.

If your setting team is made up of setters that are official gym employees, you may consider implementing various perks for them as well. Again, they do not need to be large or valuable, but adding these incentives helps to keep the setters motivated and producing as you would like them to.

## Turnover Rate

In order to allow for timely turnover of climbs, most gyms will set up some sort of system to monitor how long a given climb has been on the wall. For the majority of gyms this is as simple as writing the set date on the climb's identification tag and then stripping and replacing the climb after a certain period of time has passed. Just how long the climb should stay on the wall depends on many things, but most importantly on the size of the gym and the number of other climbs offered. The bigger the gym and the more offerings, the longer a climb can typically be left on the wall. The fewer the options, the quicker climbers will be looking for something new to climb and the more valuable the space on the wall will be. Most climbers will want to have enough time attempting the climb in order to redpoint it, if interested, and so you may need to be open to leaving a climb up for a bit of additional time if there are people still interested in working on it. Overall though, your main focus should be in making sure that there are always fresh and new options for climbers who frequent the wall. Because of this, several gyms are now adopting "expiration" dates. Quite simply this is a date written on the climb's identification tag that shows the approximate date that route will be removed. This gives climbers a clear indication of just how long they have to try and succeed on the climb.

## Difficulty Ratios and Climb Disbursement

It's the responsibility of the Head Routesetter to develop an ideal count of the total number of climbs needed in the gym. Once this total ideal number has been decided upon, the next decision needs to be how many of these should be at each difficulty level, and in what areas they should be set (bouldering, toprope or lead). While this ideal disbursement should be the loose pattern at any given time for the number of climbs in the gym, it should not necessarily be written in stone. You may need to have more climbs of a given difficulty level or style of climbing, depending on the interests and levels of those using the walls. If this is the case feel free to adjust the totals as needed, but still keep your original plan as the ideal. While it's important to cater to those climbers who frequent the gym, you should at no time neglect or alienate any of the other user groups or difficulty levels. A good question to ask yourself is: "If a group of climbers of any style and difficulty level came to my facility for the day, would there be enough options available to make the wall(s) appealing to them?" If not, you need to adjust your plan.

On a similar note try to make sure that at any given difficulty level that your facility has climbs of different styles, offered on as many different types of terrain as possible. This is why it's important to have setters on staff that have different setting styles (or are capable of more than one style). Trying to cover all the bases can be somewhat daunting, but make every effort to show diversity wherever possible.

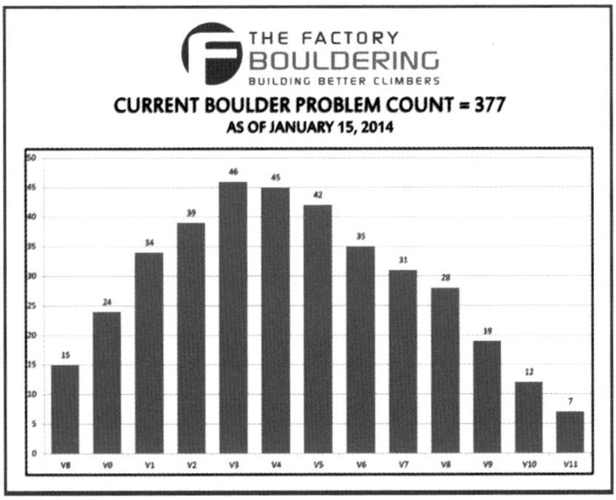

# Holds

The Head Routesetter is usually the one responsible for all things relating to holds. This encompasses many different mundane duties that aren't glamorous, but are necessary all the same. These include making sure that there are always clean holds to set with, collecting and setting aside (sorted by manufacturer) broken or defective holds for return to the manufacturer, painting off-color holds if applicable (see page 82) and keeping them organized. These duties will not necessarily be done by the Head Routesetter, but will be managed by him/her and usually delegated to setters or other staff members.

Your setters cannot set without holds. Because of this it's up to you to make sure that once holds come off the wall (or new holds are received) that they are cleaned and sorted into some sort of logical storage system. There are many different styles of hold storage, but they are usually separated into boxes or plastic storage cartons by size and/or style. If your gym sets by color (see page 52) they will need to be further broken down by color. In this way your setters can come in and be as efficient as possible with their setting time. Since many setters are compensated based on time spent setting, having an organized system in place and holds ready when they arrive will get you more climbs for the same compensation and time spent.

Most modern hold companies offer at least a limited guarantee on their holds against breakage (several offer lifetime guarantees). Because of this it's important that broken holds don't end up in the trash can. Many times a setter that breaks a hold will feel like they're going to get in trouble and try to dispose of the hold to hide the breakage. Instill in your setters the knowledge that broken holds are occasionally part of the game and that if your facility returns the hold that you can get a free replacement. At the same time educate them as to why the hold broke and try to teach them how to avoid breaking holds again in a similar situation. Often times very small holds and foot chips are not part of this guarantee program, so it's a good idea to check with the hold companies you deal with to find out the particulars of their guarantee.

Now for the fun part... The Head Routesetter will usually also be the one that places orders for new holds when the budget allows. There are a lot of different hold companies out there these days. Because of this keep your eyes open and try to get catalogs and visit websites from as many different companies as possible. Variety in your hold arsenal is very important and while there are some big companies that have great and very complete lines, there are also some very small companies that have some unique offerings. Talk to other gyms and see what they like and don't be afraid to gamble every now and again. Talk to your Gym Manager and set up some sort of regular hold budget with which to purchase holds. This may be a small dollar amount monthly, a larger amount every few months or an even larger amount every six months. Your options will be somewhat dependent on the facility's finances, but try to find a balance of regular infusions of new holds and the ability to place larger orders and capitalize on the quantity discounts offered by most hold companies.

# Feedback

Remember that the setters in your facility are a team, and as a team they need feedback in order to improve and work well together. Make sure that there is a method in place for climbers to submit comments and general feedback about the climbs your team sets. This can be as easy as a comment box or an inbox with your name on it, and regular reminders to climbers from the gym management and staff to use it.

Likewise, schedule regular meetings or group setting times where this feedback can be given back to the team as a group or individually. Be careful to not chastise anyone too harshly in a public setting, and at the same time don't hesitate to give your praise often and publicly where due. These regular team gatherings can be great morale boosters and forums for the sharing of skills and ideas. Involve as many of the setters as possible in the organization of these gatherings and be sure that everyone feels that they have merit and a voice in the overall workings of your routesetting system.

# HOLDS

There are literally thousands of holds on the market today, offered by many dozens of companies. With so many choices available it can be somewhat difficult to decide what to use. While this abundance of choices will certainly be a little overwhelming at first, it's actually a blessing for the coursesetter. This variety makes it that much easier for you to find exactly what you might need for your route, and can keep the many routes and problems in your gym diverse and interesting. Hold variety is just as important as setting variety; without either one those climbing on your creations will quickly become bored and the climbing will seem redundant.

If you're new to a certain facility and aren't familiar with its available holds, take the time to dig through the hold bins and see what's there for you to use. When you're stuck halfway through a setting session and can't find that perfect hold, you might just remember seeing one that would work and will know where to find it. You might also find inspiration while fingering the holds. Sometimes a particularly unique hold will get your imaginative juices flowing and before you know it you'll have the vision for a complete climb growing from just one hold.

# Hold Styles

All of the holds out there can be separated into three different styles. Let's make things easy and define these styles right up front. They are Training, Artistic and Rock Realistic. Training shapes are usually very clean and simple shapes that have a specific purpose and offer a comfortable and ergonomic grip. Usually they have a single usable feature and are straightforward to use. These are the bread and butter of indoor climbing and work wonderfully to isolate and strengthen specific hand and gripping positions. The second style, Artistic, describes those holds that have an abstract or creative appearance. A well thought out Artistic hold will still be very useful, but the first thing that you'll notice when looking at it is its appearance and overall design. These holds will seldom look like anything found in the natural world. Artistic holds often have less obvious gripping features and are used a fair amount in competition setting due to their hidden sweet spots and the difficulty to figure them out from the ground. Rock Realistic holds are those that mimic rock styles found at different outdoor climbing areas. These include limestone, sandstone, granite, patina and many new variations coming onto the recent market. Although these holds can often be a little more painful to climb on a daily basis, they are often the best choice when trying to replicate a specific outdoor climb on an artificial wall. They also work well for theme setting.

Regardless of the style of hold that you select, try to envision all possible ways to use the hold. Most holds will have a singular feature or sweet spot that will most commonly be the portion of the hold used by climbers. However, challenge yourself to use the hold in an orientation or way that climbers won't expect. If the hold has multiple usable features, try to make one of the lesser features the one that works best in your sequence. The more creative you can make your use of the selected holds, the more interesting and challenging the climb will be for its end users.

## Bolt On Holds

The majority of artificial holds will fall into this category. These are your traditional climbing holds, where installation is made using a single bolt through the center of the hold and into a T-nut installed in the wall panel. Occasionally holds will also have set screw holes provided on the outer end(s) to prevent them from spinning during use, but the primary attachment is made using the single bolt.

In recent years, there has been a trend towards producing larger and larger holds, commonly referred to as "features." Often these features will take the form of large slopers or shelves and will provide a degree of realism seldom found when using their smaller counterparts. While this size of hold can lend a defining character and unique usages to a climb, care must be taken in regard to their placement. Due to their size, features will sometimes get in the way of other adjacent climbs or make it difficult to see smaller holds installed in the same area as the feature. They can also block the grasping of or release of certain types of holds located close to the feature. Every effort should be made to prevent these when placing the feature.

When installing bolt on holds make sure that you are using the correct type of bolt for that hold. Some manufacturers have experimented with holds that can be installed using more than one bolt type, but most are intended to be installed with one of three types of bolts. These are the cap head (regular) bolt, the flat head (aka: taper or martini) bolt and the button head bolt. If the hold you intend to install has a fairly deep, cylindrical recess (usually 7/16" or 11/16" diameter or thereabouts) and a washer you should use a cap head bolt. If it has a tapered recess (similar to a funnel in shape) and (usually) no washer you should use a flat head bolt. These are usually found when dealing with thinner holds that do not have enough material under the washer to prevent the hold from breaking when tightened or withstanding leverage during use. The area of the flat head's contact with the hold material is considerably greater than the area of contact between the bottom of a cap head bolt's head and the top of the washer, resulting in greater load disbursement when tightening the bolt or using the hold. Finally if the washer of your hold is flush with the top of the hold (or very minimally recessed) you will probably want to use a button head bolt. This will allow for a much lower-profile projection of the bolt head from the surface of the hold and will usually prevent climbers from using the bolt head as a foot hold or thumb catch. Especially in the case of the cap and flat head bolts, using the wrong bolt type can lead to broken or spinning holds. For more info on bolt types see Tools on page 92

## SCREW ON HOLDS

In recent years a number of hold manufacturers have introduced lines of screw on holds. If you haven't yet spent time setting with screw ons, you should. Since their installation is not limited by available t-nut placements, the chances are greater that you will be able to position the hold exactly where you want it. Also, with the availability of diverse screw on offerings have come new trends in hold placement, some of which are specific to screw ons and very unique. These include placement as pinches or thumb catches on arete features, creating slots by screwing two parallel to each other (or one parallel to a bolt on hold), acting as a thumb catch for an adjacent bolt on hold, adding a more positive grasping feature on large sloping holds, etc. Likewise screw on design has allowed for longer holds types (fins, pinches and rails) that would ordinarily spin if produced with a traditional bolt on mounting system.

The original screw on hold; the jib, is still one of the most often used. A jib is basically a small (sometimes tiny) foothold that is mounted to the wall using a screw or screws. These footholds are great for setting precise footwork, demanding constant body tension and for use as supplemental or intermediate foot options. Some gyms will litter their bouldering walls with jibs and they will either be "on" for all problems, or will provide more challenging variations by using "jibs only" for footholds on a given problem.

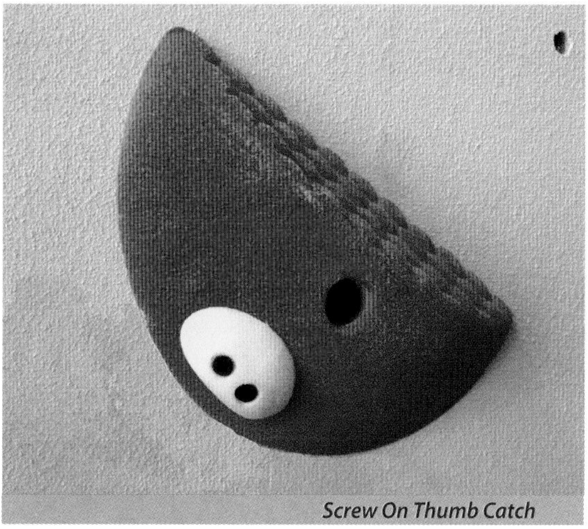

*Screw On Thumb Catch*

All screw on holds have recesses deigned for the placement of screws. Some of these are pre-drilled while others have only a small recess for the screw head to seat into. Those that do not yet have a hole through the hold will need to be drilled out. This can either be done while installing the hold (using a self-tapping screw) or with a drill bit prior to installation. In the case of holds made from flexible urethanes, you can sometimes screw right through the material without pre-drilling a hole, but be warned that some materials will crack when doing this. It's generally best to pre-drill a hole if one does not exist. You may also want to add additional screws to a hold if it does not sit flush with the wall, or if it flexes during use. When doing this make sure that you countersink the screw head to bury any sharp protrusion that might cut fingers, hands or shoe rubber. When installing screw on holds make sure to use a long enough screw. On plain plywood or texture painted walls this shouldn't be a concern, but on walls with a thick concrete or textured finish you'll want to make sure that the screw extends through this finish allowing the screw's threads to bite into the plywood beneath. You might occasionally install a screw and have it bottom out or break off before it is fully tightened. If this occurs you've probably hit a piece of steel framing behind the wall surface. You will either need to use a shorter screw or adjust your positioning slightly. When using a screw gun to install screws, make sure to set it to a low enough clutch setting to prevent the screws from breaking off due to the high torque. For more info on screws and drill bits see Tools on page 92

## Volumes

Volumes have enjoyed popularity in Europe for many years, but it's only been recently that their use has become common and popular in North America. Volumes are basically oversized holds that usually have embedded t-nuts that can be used to mount other hand holds. Their primary function is to change the angle of the wall they are mounted on. They allow for use of hold sizes and degrees of positivity that might not normally be feasible on the base wall's angle. They also introduce a more "three dimensional" movement to what would otherwise be a flat section of wall.

In some instances, such as World Cup style competition setting, the volumes themselves will be used as holds and no auxiliary holds will be attached. This type of volume setting is often the best way to replicate the compression style movement found on the larger features of natural stone.

There are a variety of volume types available. Some of them are highly featured and are usually produced in either urethane or fiberglass, while others are very simple geometric designs that can be made with the above materials or simply out of plywood panels.

Attachment is usually made by a series of set screws around the perimeter of the volume, or by a combination of mounting bolts and set screws. Some of the larger volumes on the market today come with mounting brackets that are attached to the wall. Once attached, the volumes themselves are then attached to these brackets.

## Hold Materials

Holds are made from a variety of materials, each with their own benefits and problems. The main choices have usually been polyester or polystyrene resin, polyurethane or a blend of these. There have also been a limited number of manufacturers that have chosen to use ceramics, real rock, epoxy, or a material made up of crushed rock or sand in an adhesive matrix.

Some companies use the polyester or polystyrene materials due to their lower cost. By introducing filler materials during the manufacturing process, holds made with this material can be very lightweight. The downside is that they are often more brittle (breaking easier) and can polish quicker than other hold types, leaving you with glassy smooth areas on the hold after prolonged use. They are also the harshest chemicals to work with during production and can involve more hazardous conditions for those pouring the holds. Finally, there is more of an environmental impact and concern which has limited their use more and more.

Most companies are now using polyurethane blends to make their holds. These materials are more expensive, making the holds a bit more costly, but the material offers several benefits over more traditional options. The biggest benefit is strength. Most polyurethane blend holds are considerably more difficult to break. Often times, with the softer urethanes, holds will be flexible enough to contour to match the wall's surface when installed. It's also very easy to add set screws on urethane holds, as you often won't need to pre-drill a hole for the screw. The downside with the flexible urethanes is that they can sometimes be too soft and flex while under a climbing load.

The hold surfaces generally do not polish as quickly, allowing for a longer life span from the holds.

Epoxy holds tend to be found more in European manufacturers' lines. They are generally stronger than polyester resin holds, but can suffer from many of the same disadvantages. They are often heavier than other materials as well.

The last option is more seldom used, but offers a very pleasant and cool (literally) feel when climbed on. Holds made with natural materials are making a bit of a comeback and may be seen more in years to come. One benefit of these holds is that they are less likely to polish, and if they do become too smooth, can usually be acid-etched or bead blasted to expose more texture.

## Special Characteristics

There are some special attributes to holds these days, including the following:

**Dual-texturing** – Certain portions of the hold will have a smoother surface texture (often glassy) to limit their usefulness to the climber. They are most beneficial when trying to reduce the usability of that portion of the hold for feet. Dual Tex holds offer a nice visual contrast as well.

**Hollow backs** – Many of today's larger holds are being made with a hollowed-out back. Not only does this make the hold lighter (a blessing to routesetters working on steep terrain), but it reduces the amount of material required to produce the hold, lowering the cost of the hold.

**Sliding bolts** – Often seen on longer holds such as pinches, fins, shelves and tufas. One (or multiple) mounting bolts will be positioned in a sliding recess.

Prior to the use of sliding bolts, it was next to impossible to find T-nuts in the exact location needed to use holds with multiple mounting bolts. To a certain degree, this is being replaced by the use of set screws at the ends of the hold.

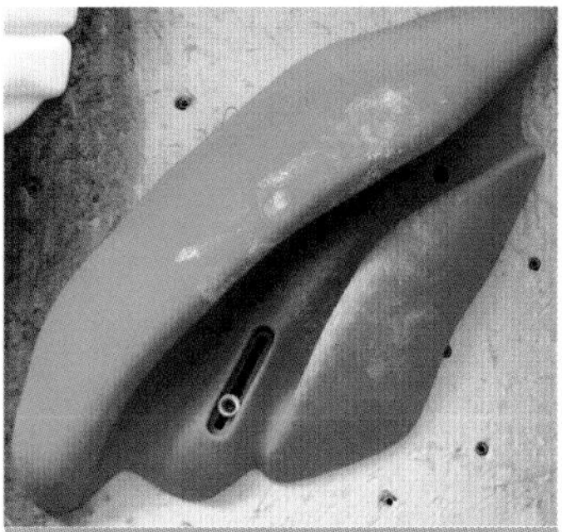

*Sliding Bolt Hole*

**Softer backing material** – Some companies are now pouring a thin layer of more flexible material on the base of their holds. This softer base allows the hold to bite to textured or uneven surfaces and drastically reduces a hold's tendency to spin. An added bonus is that it will usually prevent the edges from chipping, which often will render slopers worthless.

## Unusual Uses

Being the creative lot that we are, coursesetters have come up with some clever installation techniques that offer some unique hold usage options. Most of them require no special types of holds and can be performed on any type of climbing wall.

**Piggybacks** – Basically this is when a single hold is mounted on top of another. One method of piggybacking is to use a longer than normal mounting bolt and to run it through a second hold before inserting into the base hold. When using this method it's important to use a base hold that has a somewhat flat top surface (at least around the bolt recess) that will allow the piggybacked hold to sit flush to it. Another method of piggybacking is to use screw on holds. The obvious benefit here is that the piggybacked hold (or multiple holds) cab be attached wherever you wish. This really works best when the base hold is made from a soft enough urethane to allow the screws to bite well into the material. Think about your piggyback placement so that the resulting holes in the base hold will not make it unusable (or painful to use) on later climbs. Piggybacks can be usable holds in their own right or smaller holds that allow for good thumb catches on what would otherwise be a difficult to use hold.

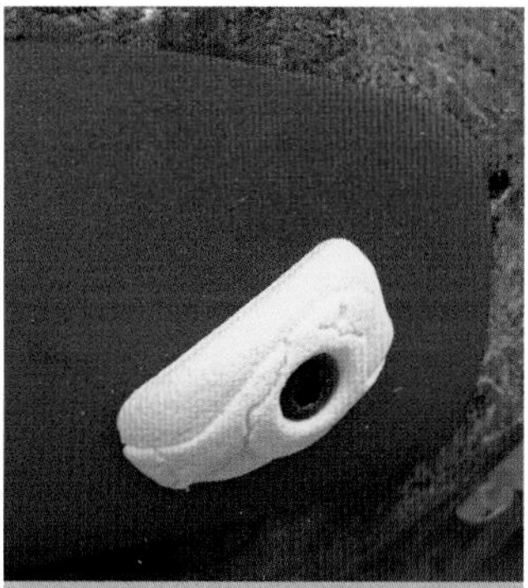

*Bolt On Piggyback*

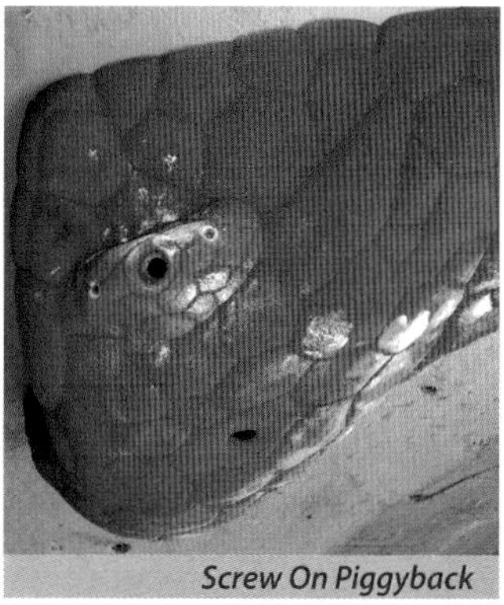

*Screw On Piggyback*

**Slots** – By installing two or more holds somewhat parallel to each other, a slot or crack feature can be created. Be sure to face the more positive portion of the holds towards each other. This method really works well when setting a target hold for a deadpoint or dyno move, as it requires more precision to hit. Some hold manufacturers offer holds specifically designed for this purpose, but you should be able to achieve adequate results with paired holds that you might already have on hand.

**Pinches** – Basically the opposite installation of slots. Install two or more holds parallel to each other, but with their most positive sides facing away from each other. By thinking about which hand the climber will grasp the pinch with, you can choose to make either the finger or the thumb side of the pinch more positive. Experiment with placing several such pinches end to end to simulate the tufa or runnel systems found on limestone.

**Rails** – By placing holds end to end you can adequately simulate rail or flake systems that can lend a more natural feel and flow to your climb. If the holds are sufficiently sized and your rail system long enough, it could also be used by the feet for heel and toe hooking as the climber progresses along the hold series.

## Cheat Proofing

Every climber brings their own rules and goals when climbing indoors. Most will acknowledge your creation and attempt to use the holds in the manner that you intended. However, there will always be that smaller contingent that looks for ways to cheat through a move or sequence. The most common ways that this can be done (other than by skipping moves) is to either use the edges of the holds or the bolt holes. It's up to an individual setter to decide whether or not they want to try to eliminate this option when setting for regular climbing use, but when setting for competitions every effort should be made to do so.

A hold's edge can often be used as a crimp or thin incut if the hold does not sit flush to the wall, or if its base has not been sanded adequately by the manufacturer. Try to be aware of this when selecting and placing your holds on the wall. For more info on how to address this see Holds That Don't Sit Flush on page 88

Dave Cepeda

Bolt holes can often provide climbers (especially those with smaller fingers) good thumb catch options or even be used as monos. These options often destroy the setter's intended hold usage (especially on sloping holds). Again, this should be taken into consideration when selecting your holds. For ways to eliminate this option see Bolt Holes on page 90

## Cleaning Holds

A big part of routesetting maintenance (especially in larger, commercial facilities) is the regular cleaning of holds. If holds are not cleaned regularly the accumulation of chalk, shoe rubber and skin oils can combine to create a veneer of polish on a hold that will render it useless. At the very least holds should be cleaned whenever they come off the wall. On more popular climbs key holds may need to be taken down, cleaned and reinstalled more regularly.

**There are basically five ways to clean your holds:**

**Sink scrubbing** – Just like it sounds. Fill the sink with a solution of warm water and cleaner and scrub. Different people swear by different cleaning agents, but whatever you use try to avoid anything too extreme or acidic and use something that has at least a mild degreasing quality. When scrubbing the holds never use a wire brush, as this will attack and polish the hold's texture. Instead use a nylon bristled brush. Letting the holds soak for awhile before cleaning them will often loosen the grime and limit the amount of "elbow grease" required to clean them.

**Dishwashers** – Many facilities have installed dishwashers for the purpose of cleaning their holds. The amount of chalk that comes off the holds during the cleaning cycle might warrant looking into getting a higher quality or more commercial machine. Basic household models often cannot handle the workload and waste that regular hold cleaning will require. Make sure to set your machine on "Pots and Pans" or a similar high-intensity cleaning option.

**Acid bath** –Another way to clean your dirty holds is in an acid solution. You will need two large containers for this method of cleaning. Most facilities use five gallon plastic buckets or larger tubs for this purpose. The first bucket is for the acid solution and the second is for a clean water rinse (to further dilute the solution and to wash away its remains). The acid used is Muriatic acid. This is available at most hardware and home improvement stores and is routinely used in the concrete, janitorial and pool industries. The bucket should be filled about halfway full **before** adding an additional inch or so of acid, resulting in an approximate 10:1 mix ratio. Dirty holds are placed in this solution for a couple of minutes before being transferred to the clean water bucket, and then finally laid out in the sun to dry. The acid solution will attack and dissolve climbing chalk and skin oils, but will not always remove shoe rubber. Larger holds or features will need to be dipped one end at a time, cleaned in larger containers or cleaned using a different method.

Muriatic acid is very strong and can potentially be dangerous. As such, there are certain precautions that should be taken when using it or its solution. Wear clothing that covers exposed skin areas as exposure to the acid or its solution can cause chemical burns. Use gauntlet-style, acid-resistant gloves and eye protection when working with the acid solution. Use only in well ventilated areas. Always add acid to water when making the solution; **never** add water directly to acid as it can cause a reaction that releases toxic gases into your breathing environment and can burn your eyes. Finally, do not mix Muriatic acid (or its solution) with any other chemicals.

The acid solution can often be used for several cleaning sessions (especially if not too many holds have been cleaned). Put a tight lid on the solution bucket and make sure that it is marked clearly so that no one mistakes its contents for water. The bucket can then be set aside for future reuse.

The biggest downside to using acid is the question of what to do with the dirty solution when it's no longer usable. Many people further dilute it with water before dumping it down the drain, while others just dump it straight away. Either method has potential environmental concerns.

**Vinegar Bath** – An alternative to the Acid Bath option, is to do something similar with vinegar. The acidic quality of the vinegar dissolves the base material of climbing chalk and works very well.

Instead of mixing an acid solution, simply fill the first container to the desired level with undiluted White Vinegar. Place the holds in this bath for a few minutes before transferring to a clean water rinse in a separate container. In most cases only a mild amount of scrubbing will be required. Generally all but the toughest accumulation of shoe rubber will come off with just a few minutes immersion in the vinegar.

**Pressure Washer** – This method requires an outdoor area or a large room with a floor drain. Dirty holds are either laid out on the ground or placed on a screened rack. A power washer is then used to spray the chalk and grime off the holds. This is a messy process, but one that is used by many facilities with good results.

Another similar option is to take your dirty holds to a self-service car wash, where higher strength power wash wands (often with various cleaning solution options) are available. The obvious downside to this option is the transporting of the holds there and back.

## Painting Holds

Many facilities have chosen to set their climbs using colored holds. When ordering in large enough quantities, most hold companies will make an effort to match the colors used by your facility if you let them know when placing your order. Often times though, you will end up with off-color holds or color variations that are not distinguishable or uniform enough for use in this system. Spray painting the holds is your best option at this point.

When painting holds there are a few things to consider and keep in mind. Once you have decided that you are willing to paint holds try to select bright, recognizable colors. Avoid color variations (light, medium or dark of the same color) as this will only lead to climber confusion and a less appealing visual presentation. When determining what color to paint a given hold, try to select a color that is similar to its original. This will require less paint to do the job and the hold will maintain more of its original surface texture.

In general painting holds should be done minimally, but if you have holds of varying shades and want to standardize coloration it can be done with good results if you are delicate in your approach. When painting, do not get too close to the hold and apply in several thin coats versus a single heavy coat. Finally, use less paint in the usable area of the hold; focus most of your painting on the more visible and less-often used parts of the hold. Again the reasoning here is to try to maintain as much texture on the hold as possible. You will undoubtedly lose some texture by painting, but not too much.

## Fine Tuning

You will sometimes want to use a hold that has a too rough texture, or that has a blemish or air bubble in a key spot. These are very easy things to fix, and by doing so you'll end up with a hold that is much more comfortable to use.

**Texture** – If a hold has a texture that is too rough for your liking, it can be sanded using 100-grit sandpaper. With just a few swipes of the paper you can drastically smooth the texture. Be careful though, as it's very easy to sand off too much of the texture, resulting in too smooth of a finish.

**Blemishes** – There are two types of blemishes that will affect the usage of a hold. The first is a protruding bump (often sharp). These are usually caused when the manufacturer's mold starts to deteriorate. They can usually either be cut off with a sharp knife or ground down by rubbing that portion of the hold against a concrete sidewalk or coarse sandpaper. If the blemish is located inside a pocket or incut feature where it cannot be accessed easily, you may need to use a Dremel® tool or other handheld grinder.

The second type of blemish is an air bubble or other recessed void in the surface texture. These are caused when air is trapped inside the mold during the manufacturing process. Often simply sanding (softening) the sharp edges of the recess will make it comfortable enough to use. If this does not prove sufficient (or if the recess is overly large), a quick drying filler material (such as Bondo®) can be used to fill the void. This filler material should then be sanded to provide a smooth transition to the surrounding area.

## Hold Preservation

Today's holds are more expensive than older versions, primarily because the urethanes used in the industry currently are more costly than older materials. With many companies now outsourcing the production of their holds, you are often paying an increase also to cover the profit margins of these production houses. With this increase in cost comes the need to think about a hold's longevity in order to keep from needing to spend valuable budget dollars on replacing them. There are a few things you can do while setting that will drastically affect a hold's lifespan.

**Orientation** – Much of the damage done to a hold is caused by its use as a foothold. The constant rotating pressure of foot usage wear down the texture faster than anything else and will often leave you with a polished surface that's much more difficult to grasp and use with your hands. To limit this damage, consider orienting the hold so that later use as a foothold will have the climber stepping on a portion of the hold that is not normally used as a handhold. Sometimes a slight rotation of the hold in question will allow you to still use the hold as a handhold with the same basic effect, but allow foot usage to occur elsewhere on the hold.

**Placement on the wall** – Especially when setting boulder problems, using a larger and more expensive hold higher on the wall (especially within a body length of the top or finishing hold) will mean that it will not get used as a foothold, allowing the texture to last dramatically longer than placements where it would also be used as a foothold.

**Rope wear** – On roped climbing walls, be aware of how the rope will run over the section of wall (and your hold) while climbing past it during a lead climb or while lowering off of the route. If the rope runs over your hold, consider changing its placement to prevent the rope from cutting a groove into the hold. Likewise be careful not to position incut holds to wear the rope can get caught behind and cause wear to the interior portion of the hold.

**Cleaning** – Once an accumulation of chalk builds up on a hold, the combination of body oils, sweat, foot usage and the chalk itself can create a polishing effect on the surface of the hold that is often difficult to clean off. Regular brushing or other cleaning of the holds will limit this. Encourage your facility's climbers to brush holds when this chalk buildup occurs and talk to your management about providing pole mounted brushes for climbers to use for cleaning hard to reach holds.

# TROUBLESHOOTING

**Stuck Holds**

Everyone will encounter this at some point during his or her setting experience. This usually occurs when a mounting bolt becomes cross-threaded or the hold is partially mounted when the T-nut pushes out of the rear of the wall panel. There are a few ways to address this problem, depending on the situation at hand.

If the T-nut has pushed out of the back of the wall panel (or if the T-nut is cross threaded early enough in the installation to allow for the T-nut to be pushed out of the back of the wall panel) another setter or helper can go behind the wall and firmly grasp the T-nut with

a pair of pliers or Vise Grips®. Once your helper has a good grip on the T-nut you will be able to loosen the hold with your mounting wrench. The damaged T-nut should be replaced with a new T-nut and the hold can then be installed. If the t-nut cannot be grasped, you may need to use an angle grinder to cut off the back flange of the t-nut. Make sure to cut through the barrel of the t-nut above the radius that joins the barrel to the base flange of the t-nut. You will also be cutting through the mounting bolt. Once cut all the way through, the remaining pieces of bolt and t-nut can be pushed through the hole. Depending on how much damage has been done to the plywood or wall panel you may be able to install another t-nut right away. If the plywood has been damaged, cut a small piece of plywood (maybe three inches square or a similar sized triangle) and drill a hole in the center. Install a t-nut in the hole and line it up with the existing t-nut hole and mount your plywood patch to the rear surface of the wall panel.

Another fix comes into play if you do not have a helper, cannot reach the rear of the wall or the T-nut cannot be pushed out of the back of the wall panel. First try using a ratchet handle (see Tools on page 92) with a long handle. Sometimes the extra leverage gained by using this teo try and loosen the hold is enough to get the hold off. If you're successful with this, you'll need to re-tap the t-nut or replace it with a new one.

If you are unable to remove the hold using a ratchet this more drastic measures must be taken. You will need to place a crowbar or the claws of a hammer between the stuck hold and the wall panel surface. While levering out on the hold loosen the bolt using your mounting wrench. This can sometimes be a little difficult to start and you may need a helper to do the levering while you loosen the bolt. Be forewarned though that this creates a lot of force and that when the bolt releases from the t-nut the hold (and possibly you and your helper) will go flying away from the wall. Be careful! Often the T-nut can be rethreaded using a tap (see section below). If this is not possible the T-nut should be replaced. In cases where this will not work, or if there is not enough room to insert something behind the hold to provide leverage, a reciprocating saw or hacksaw can be used to cut the mounting bolt between the rear of the hold and the face of the climbing wall panel. Be careful to cut in a controlled manner to limit damage to the wall panel surface. In the most extreme situations, a angle grinder can be used to cut the head of the bolt off. This should be the last resort, as you will destroy the hand hold during the removal process. It still may be preferable to possibly damaging the wall panel surface though.

## Cross Threaded T-nuts

If you are setting and come across a cross-threaded T-nut it will need to be re-tapped prior to use. This is easily achieved using a 3/8"-16 metal tap (see Tools on page 92). This is a threaded tool that is designed to repair and re-cut threads into a T-nut or other metal hole. It's far preferable to use a tap mounted in a manual handle as opposed to installing the tap into your power drill, because the power drill creates more than enough torque to weld the tap into the T-nut or to break the tap itself.

First blow or brush all dust and debris out of the T-nut hole. Next begin slowly, but firmly threading the tap into the damaged T-nut. When you start to meet with resistance turn the tap, another partial turn and then unthread the tap allowing the cut metal shavings to fall (or be blown) out of the hole. Begin threading the tap in again and repeat the process until the tap turns freely and the threads have been re-cut into the T-nut. Don't force it; you're cutting metal, but at the same time too much pressure can damage the tap or push the T-nut out of the back of the wall panel. Be patient!

Finally, take a look at the mounting bolt that you were using when you discovered your t-nut was damaged. Are the threads in good condition or are the first few threads flattened and wider than normal? If the threads are damaged, it's best to just through the bolt away. Using a bolt with damaged threads will only damage the t-nut again. If your damaged bolt is a long enough (and expensive enough) one that you would rather not throw it away, you can cut off the damaged threads and continue using the bolt. If your cut is not a nice and clean one, you may need to run the bolt though a 3/8-16" die (see Tools on page 92) to clean up the leading edge of the threads. You may also want to slightly bevel the tip of the cut bolt with an angle grinder to eliminate the sharp edges and to allow for easier insertion into t-nuts.

## HOLDS THAT EXTEND BEYOND EDGE OF WALL PANEL

You will sometimes find the perfect hold only to discover that once it's installed its edge extends beyond the edge of the wall panel. This can be bad in two ways. First of all it usually allows for another hold option other than the one desired. Secondly the use of the protruding portion can cause a dangerous amount of leverage to occur against the mounting bolt, possibly causing a broken hold. There are a few ways to address this if you aren't willing to find another hold: install a new T-nut or break out the grinder. Sometimes installing a new T-nut (see Tools on page 92 a few inches further away from the edge will allow you to use the desired hold. If this is not an option the edge of the hold can be ground down using a power grinder to prevent the extension of the hold. This is a drastic measure that would probably only be suitable for a competition environment, as it will permanently alter the hold. Be careful when grinding that you do not leave any sharp edges that will act as a painful thumb catch or might possibly cut into shoe rubber. If neither of these options is desirable you can also tape over the offending edge using a length of your marking tape. If you are dealing with a large protrusion you may also want to write "off" or "do not use" on the tape to further discourage use.

A similar circumstance is encountered when the desired hold will not fit into an inside corner feature. Again either a new T-nut can be installed or the edge of the hold ground down to allow it to fit into the area.

## HOLDS THAT DON'T SIT FLUSH

Usually because of an uneven wall surface, but also occasionally due to a T-nut that was not installed perpendicular to the wall surface; you will get a hold that does not sit entirely flush to the wall. This is not usually a concern as long as the hold can be mounted securely to the wall without the fear of it spinning. However, occasionally the hold will sit at such an angle to the wall that one of the outer edges will lift away from the wall creating a "cheater crimp." If you want to avoid this there are a couple of ways to address the lifted edge. The simplest fix (if the condition is a result of a crooked T-nut) is to insert a small setting wrench into the T-nut and lever it into a perpendicular position, allowing the hold to be installed parallel to the wall surface. If it's more than a T-nut issue, and for a short-term fix that would be more conducive to a competition environment, you can simply take a length of your marking tape and tape over the lifted edge. If you choose to address the edge in this manner make sure that you do not affect the usable portion of the hold with your tape placement and that it is positioned in such a way that it will withstand repeated foot and hand traffic. Another option is to install a set screw (see paragraph below for technique) on the lifted portion of the hold to draw it tight to the wall surface. It's generally far easier to install this set screw and draw the hold to the wall surface before you completely tighten the hold's mounting bolt. If the set screw is not sufficient to draw that edge of the hold tight to the wall surface you can also shim the opposite side of the hold with some sort of hard spacer material roughly equivalent to the thickness of the gap that you are trying to close on the lifted edge. If the gap is a result of the hold's base not being sanded uniformly, you may also be able to sand the base further with a power sander.

## Holds That Spin or Are Likely To Spin

Occasionally a hold will need to be positioned in such a way that it could spin when used. This can be caused by one of two things: either an uneven wall surface where the hold will not make even contact or the use of a hold where the usable feature is located at the outer end of the hold, far from the mounting bolt. Of the most concern are situations where the usable portion of the hold is positioned to the left of the mounting bolt or when the force of use would move the hold in a counter-clockwise rotation. Because of this orientation the mounting bolt will loosen when the hold spins. If the hold will possibly spin clockwise there is less of a concern, as this will actually tighten the mounting bolt further.

There are a couple of ways to address a spinning hold. The first is to use a set screw. Many hold manufacturers now offer small divots molded into their holds to accept set screws (especially on their larger holds or long shapes that would be more prone to spinning). If there is no divot (or if the divot has no hole through the hold), pre-drill a 3/16" hole through the hold before installing the set screw. If you are using a urethane hold this may not be necessary, as you may be able to install the set screw directly through the material using a power drill or screw gun. Be careful though, as some rigid urethanes will crack if you do not pre-drill a hole. The set screw should be positioned in a place on the hold that would support the hold in the direction of its likely spinning. You should try to make sure that the head of the set screw is below the surface of the hold to prevent catching a finger or thumb on a protruding edge. This is easily achieved by using a countersink type drill bit or by reaming out the outer edge of the drilled hole to allow the screw to suck into the hold further during installation. Again with a urethane hold this may not be necessary, as the material is often soft enough to allow the screw to suck into the hold without creating a recess.

The other method of addressing a potentially spinning hold is to place a small foot chip, mounting bolt or screw under the edge of the hold on the side that it would spin toward. This is commonly referred to as a "block." If there happens to be a T-nut hole located in the proper spot, a low profile foot chip will accomplish this just fine. However, the likelihood of an open T-nut hole being positioned properly to match your desired hold orientation is not high. The same effect can be achieved by installing a wood screw under the edge of the hold. Try to install the screw at an upward 45-degree angle to eliminate leaving the sharp edges of the screw head exposed.

*Set Screw*

## Bolt Holes

Bolt holes can often provide climbers (especially those with smaller fingers) good thumb catch options or even be used as monos. These options often destroy the setter's intended hold usage (especially on sloping holds). This should be taken into consideration when selecting your holds. If you have found the perfect hold and would like to limit a climber's ability to use the bolt hole, there are a few ways to address the problem.

**Cover It** – Take a piece of marking tape and cover over the bolt hole. This really only works well with extremely sticky tape and on holds that have a smooth surface texture around the bolt hold. As such, this method should be limited to competition use as any prolonged usage will undoubtedly cause the tape to peel off.

**Label It** – Add a label at the beginning of the climb (or adjacent to the hold, written on a piece of marking tape) saying "No Bolt Holes" or "Bolt Holes Off."

**Stuff It** – The bolt hole can be filled with wadded up climbing or marking tape. The downside of this method is that it's often difficult to extract all of the tape in order to remove the bolt or tighten the hold. You can make this easier by using a single long piece of tape to fill the hole. This way once you get a portion of the tape removed you'll be guaranteed that you can pull the remaining tape out since it's one continuous piece.

**Washer It** – By using an extra washer on top of the bolt hole recess (use a small enough diameter washer so that it spans over the recess, but does not extend out far enough to affect the use of the hold) and then install a longer bolt through this washer and into the T-nut. Ideally you'll want to use a button head bolt when using this method to avoid adding a good thumb catch or foothold option, but when using this method on higher profile holds you may not have a button head bolt long enough.

*Washer It*

# TOOLS

## Wrenches

There are two sizes of wrenches used for routesetting. These are the 7/32″ and 5/16″ Allen key wrenches. There are a few different styles regularly used:

**L Wrenches** – These small wrenches used to come with hold sets in the old days. They're really only good to have around for back up wrenches as the arms are not long enough to provide enough leverage for most situations. If you set in an older gym that has been retrofit with one of the thicker, modern flooring systems, you may have some t-nuts that are very close to the top surface of the flooring. These shorter handled wrenches are sometimes good for tightening and loosening holds in these lower t-nuts also.

**T Wrenches** – Commonly called "T handles," these are the most common style of wrench used in routesetting. These have a "t" shape allowing for better and more comfortable leverage options. They also have a longer main arm, allow for much less awkward usage. The regular lengths work well for almost all holds, however there are some manufacturer's whose larger holds have deeply recessed bolt holes that necessitate the use of the longer model(s).

**Ratchet Handles** – One of the best choices for volume setting. A ratchet handle (usually associated with socket set use) is fitted with an Allen key head of the appropriate size. The use of this tool's ratcheting feature greatly speeds up the installation and removal of holds and saves your wrist the stress of repeated

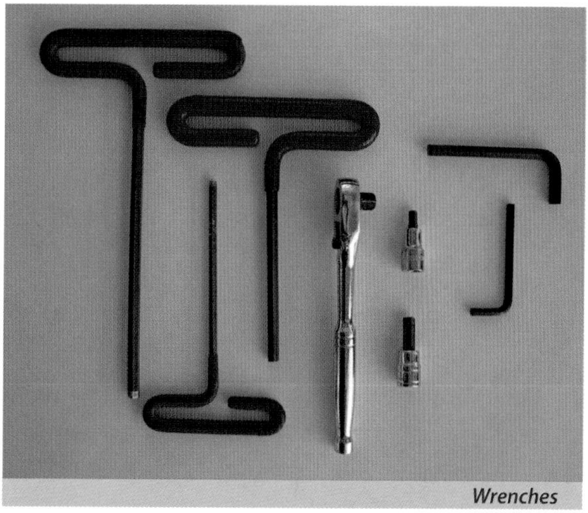

*Wrenches*

twisting. You will usually also get better leverage when using a ratchet instead of a traditional T handle.

## Impact Drivers

These are fast becoming the tool of choice with most setters. In the hands of a skilled setter they can drastically speed up the setting process. They also help to prevent wrist and other similar injuries that can sometimes occur as a result of turning a wrench repeatedly. This doesn't mean that they are the right tool for everyone though. Using them takes a certain amount of skill and attention. Because of the power associated with the impact, it's VERY easy to cross thread bolts when using them. Many gyms do not allow their use and most Head Setters require their setters to use other types of wrenches until a certain level of experience is achieved.

*Impact Driver and Attachments*

When using impacts to install holds, be very careful to ensure that your mounting bolt is lined up straight with the t-nut. You should then slowly pull the trigger without pushing too hard on the drill itself. This will give the bolt a chance to engage with the t-nut threads before too much pressure is introduced. Once the bolt has started, you can then spin the drill faster and push. This will become second nature, but definitely reduces the number of cross threads you'll encounter when using impacts to set.

Often you will want to change sizes of tips in your impact. If you've been using one size for some time, it may be difficult to remove the first tip from your tool. Firmly striking the end of the tip against something hard (the ground, a ladder rung, etc.) will usually loosen the tip and make it easier to remove.

If for whatever reason you choose not to use an impact when setting, you should certainly consider them the tool of choice when stripping holds off the wall. An impact with a fully-charged battery will make this much-dreaded process far more efficient.

## Tap

Used to rethread stripped T-nuts. Consists of a handle and a 3/8" x 16 threads per inch tap. For use directions (see Cross Threaded T-nuts on page 87). Occasionally setters will insert the tap into a drill motor and sometimes this works well, but it will often break the tap or it will get stuck in the T-nut due to the additional torque created when using a power tool. It's generally far better to use the manual handle that is often sold with the tap.

## Die

Used to clean up and/or re-cut threads on damaged or cut mounting bolts. If the threads are not too badly damaged you can simply thread the die onto the end of the bolt. If the threads are badly damaged, you may need to clamp the bolt into a vise or have someone else hold it with pliers while you tighten the die onto the bolt and repair the threads.

## T-Nuts

*Screw In* *Concrete Wall Pallet Nut* *Hammer In*

**Hammer In** – Most home gyms and lower-budget climbing facilities will use this type of T-nut. It is hammered into the rear of the plywood sheathing and is anchored with a series of prongs (usually 3 to 5) that extend from the base of the T-nut into the plywood. The biggest benefit in using these is their simple installation and lower cost. The downside is that they can often be pushed out of the plywood when a bolt becomes cross threaded and the fact that they can usually only be rethreaded once or twice because of the thinner metal thickness. To help secure these to the back of the wall panels, you can install at least two short wood screws into the v-shaped grooves at the base of the prongs to keep the t-nuts from turning or pushing out.

**Screw In** – There are a variety of screw in T-nut models. All of them are hammered into the rear of the plywood sheathing and are initially kept in place by friction between the T-nut's barrel and the plywood. Set screws are then installed through the T-nut's base into the plywood, usually through holes in the base plate or notches in the outer edge of the base plate. The obvious benefit here is that they cannot be easily pushed out of the rear of the wall panel during use. The thicker and more expensive models can usually be rethreaded several times.

Both types of t-nuts are available with longer barrels and you will usually see these in use on walls that have a thick concrete or other surface texture to bring the front of the t-nut closer to the surface of the wall. In these situations, the longer barrels allow you to set with shorter bolts than you otherwise would need to.

## Tape

**Duct** – Available in several colors, this is the most common type of tape used for marking climbs. Make sure that you are using higher-quality tape as it's considerably sticker than less expensive brands. Most gyms use either the 1" or 2" widths.

**Gaffer's** – This cloth tape is also available in several colors and is used in the entertainment industry. It can often be a little more expensive, but generally it's very durable and adhesive. Most gyms use the 1" width.

*Czar Goss*

**Masking** – As a budget option, colored masking tape can be used to mark climbs. There are some climbing specific manufacturers that offer pattered masking tape. This type of tape works best on smooth plywood or painted finish walls.

## Tags

**Laminated** – Made from colored and patterned paper and then laminated. Gyms using this style of tags usually buy a craft-sized laminator machine and make tags as needed at their facility.

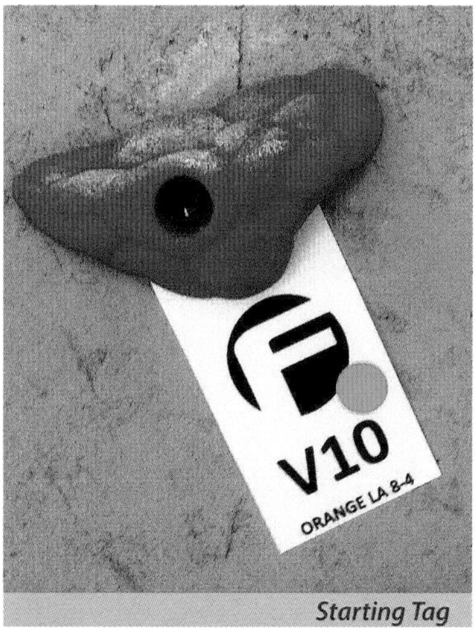


*Starting Tag*

**Plastic** – Some facilities use very thin, colored, plastic sheeting strips for marking tags.

**Ribbon** – A simple solution is to use colored fabric ribbon under your holds. This only really works well on slightly overhung and lesser-angled walls, as on steeper angles the ribbon hangs away from the hold and wall and is more difficult to easily recognize.

# Bolts

**Cap Head** – The most common type of mounting bolt used for climbing holds.

**Flat Head (aka Martini)** – Used in holds that often have no washer and an inverted funnel-shaped recess. This bolt type is usually used on thinner holds.

**Button Head** – Mounting bolt with a dome-shaped head. Used on holds where the washer is at the surface of the hold or recessed very slightly. These types of bolts are often not used as much on newer hold designs.

**Eye Bolts** – A normal 3/8" diameter, coarse-threaded eyebolt will thread into t-nuts. If you are going to be setting on roped climbing walls, it's nice to have one or two of these on hand in your setting kit. They provide a quick and easy way to hang your hold bucket or other tools on the wall, to add a directional anchor to keep you in location away from the natural line of the rope you're attached to, or to screw into a t-nut on a volume to make it easier to haul up the wall and maneuver into place.

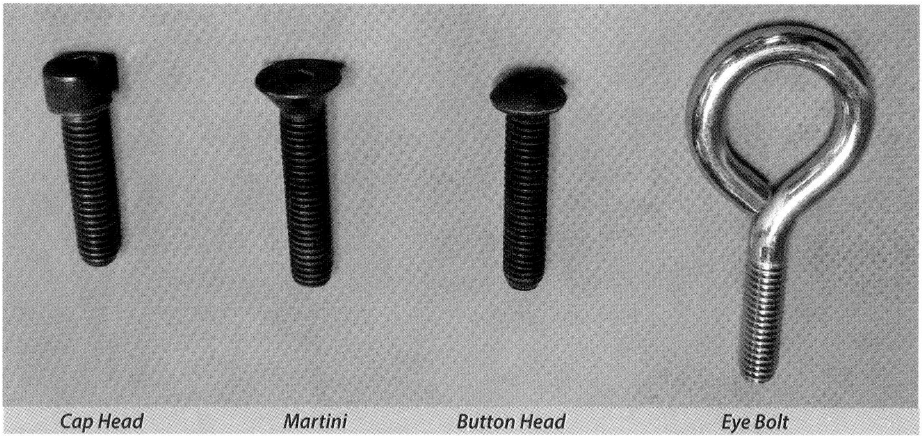

*Cap Head* *Martini* *Button Head* *Eye Bolt*

# Set Screws

**Self Tapping** – Used when the set screw hole is not yet drilled out. Due to their finer thread pattern they do not grab as well into plywood sheathing.

**Pointed tip** – The screw of choice for screw on hold installations and set screws. Use a #6 or #8 diameter, coarse-threaded screw. The black-colored drywall screws tend to be somewhat brittle and are prone to snapping during installation. Instead buy the gold-colored ones or those intended for exterior deck installations.

Either type of screw should have a bugle shaped head. The most popular versions have either a traditional Phillips or Torx pattern, with the Torx gaining popular due to a better connection between the screw tip and the screw. This better connection means less stripping of the screw head pattern, easier installation and longer screw life.

## Screw gun

A cordless screw gun or other drill motor is handy when installing set screws or screw on holds. Be sure to set the clutch setting (if possible) to a lower setting to limit the amount of torque transferred to the screw. A tool with too much torque will snap set screws very easily. These also make for very fast hold stripping tools by inserting an Allen key attachment into the drill. These can either be store bought or an old T wrench can be cut into enough pieces to make four or five suitably sized pieces.

Many setters and setting teams no longer use screw guns, having replaced them entirely with Impact Drivers. The only down side of using an impact is that traditional drill bits will not work with them. Some people opt to purchase more expensive drill bits that are designed to be used in impacts, but some may prefer to keep a normal drill on hand if for no other reason than drilling holes.

## Marking Pens

**Permanent** - Sharpies® or other permanent markers are best for identification tags, directional labels and making patterns on marking tape. These come in assorted colors.

**Paint Pens** – Paint pens come in several colors and are handy when having to make patterns or write on darker-colored tape. The white pens usually show up the best on most dark colors.

# Drill Bits

**Set Screws** – A 3/16" drill bit works well for drilling set screw holes into holds. This may be slightly oversized, but that's preferably to a tight hole. You don't want the screw to bite into the hold much before screwing into the wall. If this happens the screw can sometimes snap due to the binding created.

**Countersink** – If installing set screws into a harder material hold, you may need to drill a countersunk recess for the screw head to seat into. You can either use a special countersink bit (designed for wood working) or a conical metal countersink bit.

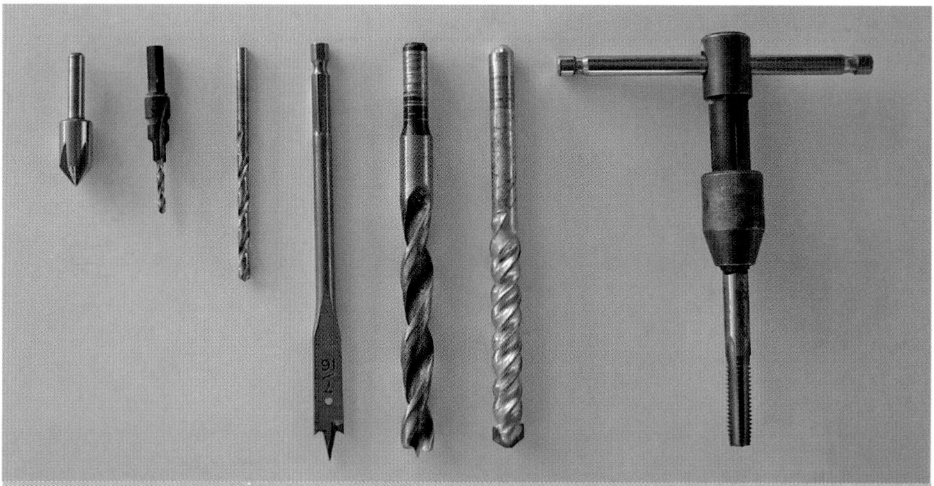

*L to R: 2 types of countersinks, 3/16" bit, t-nutting bits, and a tap and handle*

**T-nutting** – The type of T-nut that you will be installing will determine the size of hole you'll want to drill. If you are using hammer in T-nuts, drill a 7/16" hole. This is slightly undersized and will allow greater friction and less likelihood of the T-nut pushing out of the back of the wall during use. If you are going to be using a screw in T-nut, a half inch hole should be drilled. If your facility has a concrete wall finish, you may need to drill with two different bits. The first bit would be a ½" masonry bit. This should be used to drill through the concrete texture and also through the underlying metal lath (if installed). If you do not drill through the lath as well, your second bit will dull much faster. The second bit required would be a standard ½" wood bit. This will be used to drill all the way through the remainder of the wall. The best wood bits to use are a brad point bit or a less expensive paddle type bit.

## Sandpaper

Used to lessen the texture on rougher-surfaced holds. 100-grit sandpaper usually works well. This is something that is not done too often in commercial setting. Generally an overall rough texture can mean a longer hold lifespan. Rough holds will often also feel just fine once they have a liberal amount of chalk on them. That said, home wall owners and other facilities that do not get the same level of traffic may be interested in doing this to limit skin damage and extend their training sessions. Occasionally you will also get a hold that has a blemish or rough patch on it. Sandpaper will usually do the trick to make it friendlier. Be careful not to sand too much as it doesn't take too many swipes to achieve the desired effect. Once the texture is gone – you can't put it back.

## Spray Paint

Used to paint off color holds when setting using the colored holds system. Do not get too close to the hold while painting and paint with several light coats versus one heavy coat. Try to select bright primary colors that are easily distinguished from others.

## Ladders

**A Frame** – Good for setting the beginning of roped climbs and for setting boulder problems. Usually stable up to the 12-foot height. Higher models than this they can be somewhat less secure. If your budget allows invest in a higher rated, fiberglass, double-step ladder. This type of ladder has usable rungs on both sides of the ladder and is considerably more stable and comfortable to set off. Double steps also tend to last a lot longer than other A frames.

**Extension** – Used for setting taller climbs. Fiberglass ladders are the most stable, however they are very expensive and tend too be prohibitively heavy at times. A higher rated aluminum ladder will usually still be somewhat rigid and will be much easier to move around.

If your facility has any of the newer thicker foam flooring systems, with a vinyl tarp covering, you will need to place the feet of your ladder on a plank or sheet of something fairly rigid to disperse the load of the ladder and prevent damage to the vinyl top sheet. If your setting ladders are always used for setting, a practical solution is to cut a thin oval (rounded corners keep the edges from digging in) plywood plank and screw this to the bottom of the ladders feet. Doing this makes moving the ladder around far more efficient, as you do not need to position the plank independent from the ladder.

## Roped Setting Tools

There are several more ordinary climbing items that may come in handy when setting off a rope or high on ladders. These include harnesses, slings, quickdraws, carabiners (including some locking), shoulder bags or buckets, daisy chains, etriers (aiders), bolt hangers, extra mounting bolts, ascenders, FIFI or other hooks, GRI-GRI® devices, etc. There are a variety of rigging options available and far too many different systems to properly cover in this text. You should also consider adding leashes to any tools that do not have a direct clip in point to prevent you from dropping them.

## Setter's Kit

When traveling to another facility than your own to set, it's nice to carry a small setter's kit. This should include all basic items that you might need. The exact inclusions will depend on your own preferences, but most will include wrenches, a ratchet or an impact (with extra battery and charger), sandpaper, a small assortment of screws, a tap and handle, a marking pen, a handful of jibs and some extra hammer in T-nuts. Some setters may also prefer to bring their own cordless screw gun, ladders, crash pad, hold brush, etc.

Kelly Starke

# SETTING FOR COMPETITIONS

There are a variety of tactics and techniques that should be kept in mind when setting for competitions. Most carry over to regular setting situations; some are specific to competitions. There is perhaps no other time that your climbs will be subjected to as much scrutinization. As such, take your time and make every effort to insure that your competition climbs include the best setting that you have to offer.

## Variety

Make sure that the total group of climbs that will be part of the competition show a good variety of climbing styles in each difficulty level. There are many considerations when trying to achieve this variety. One consideration is the type of holds used on the climb. Make sure that you have a good offering in all of the main hold types (incuts, slopers, pinches, pockets, edges, crimps, etc.). Another thing to be aware of is that there are climbs that cover the three main types of climbing (see Styles of Climbs on page 133), as well as different lengths of climbs. Some of these could involve lengthy traverses to help add a pump before a particular section of climbing, or to make use of existing traverse walls in the gym. Try to spread competitors out throughout the facility to prevent logjams and crowds at particular sections of the gym by setting climbs of the same difficulty in different areas of the gym. Also try to make sure that you include steepness diversity by incorporating different wall angles throughout the difficulty levels. Remember that hard climbs don't need to be steep and that easier climbs don't need to be limited to the lower-angled walls. Likewise, make sure that some of the easier climbs use small holds and that some of the harder ones features large holds coupled with difficult transitions from hold to hold. The style of movement on the climbs should also vary. Make sure that you have some nice technical and static climbs as well as some truly dynamic climbs. The latter can either feature a series of deadpoints or a singular long dynamic movement. You may also want to include somewhat reachy problems and some scrunchy problems; however neither of these should decide the winner of the competition. Make sure that for every height dependent climb offered that there are several others at the same level that are not height dependent. This will make it less likely that a tall (or short) person will be unduly handicapped. Finally, don't be afraid to incorporate some "gimmick" climbs that feature alternative styles. These can include sections of campusing, jump starts, run and jumps, knee bars, figure-4's, sideways dynos and anything else you might be able to think up. By doing your best to provide this variety you will make sure that you are not favoring or hurting any single competitor's chances of success by having too many or too few climbs of a given style. If the competition's climbs are to remain on the walls after the competition, this also gives the regular wall customers a greater variety to enjoy after the fact and lessens the burden to the regular route setting duties often required to get back to a full selection of climbs in the gym.

Pat Bagley

## Difficulty

Generally competition climbs will have a gradually increasing difficulty level as the climber progresses towards the end of the climb. This helps to insure that only the better climbers will gain the finish. Many setters will build mini cruxes (of a lesser difficulty level) into a couple of spots lower on the climb. Not only does this help to "thin out the herd," but also gives the competitors a feeling of triumph as they progress through them, keeping their morale and excitement levels high.

While every effort should be made to make sure that your climbs are accurately graded, don't get too hung up on making them "perfectly graded." As you are setting it's often difficult to factor in your own fatigue and any personal strengths and weaknesses that might cloud your interpretation of the climb's true difficulty. These factors are a large reason for the entire forerunning process and usually any glaring rating errors will be found at that stage. Even at that point though, the realization must be made that there will more than likely be some climbs that are rated too easily or too difficult. This is hard to avoid entirely and will not give undue advantage to the competitors, as they will all have the same advantage or disadvantage that a sandbag or giveaway will present. This is usually more of a problem when a routesetter is setting outside his comfort range. The main importance is to make sure that competition climbs given the same rating or points value will be of comparable difficulty and that this difficulty (and the difficulty of climbs both easier and more difficult) remain consistent throughout all competition offerings. Of course as the level of competition increases (and the total number of climbs offered decreases) the importance of climbs being graded accurately also increases. Accuracy in difficulty is most important when setting climbs that will be a part of semi-final or final rounds.

## Advance Setting

When having to set competition climbs early enough before the competition that they will need to be removed and then reset on the wall, or when setting competition finals' climbs that will not be on the wall(s) during earlier competition rounds, there are a few ways to save time when they are re-established prior to the competition. Due to the additional work involved in any of these methods, it's best not to set early enough before the event to necessitate these methods. Sometimes, however, it's unavoidable and for that reason we will discuss these options:

The first method involves making a small alignment mark on the handhold and a correlating mark on the climbing wall surface (see picture) to show its proper orientation on the wall. Once you are done setting your climb (and it has been forerun) you can simply loosen the hold and rotate it to hide its true orientation from the competitor "lookie-loos" that will invariably wander in prior

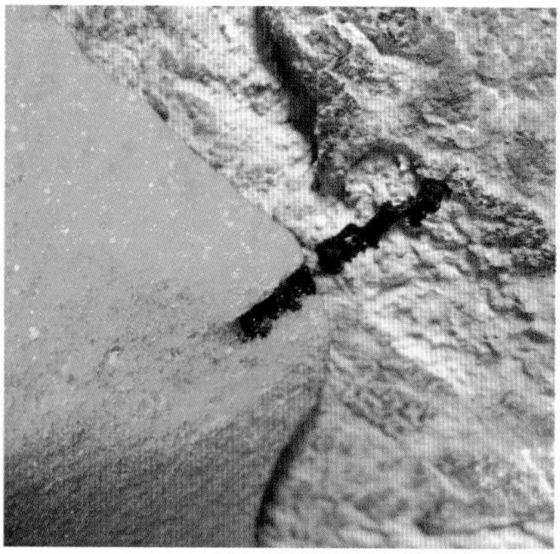

to the competition. Care must be taken to not reuse these turned holds for another problem unless they are also to be used in the original orientation. It's often a good idea to also add extra unmarked holds scattered throughout the area of your climb to further confuse competitors trying to decipher the climb prior to its use.

A variation to this method is to make the marks on the hold, but then to draw a map of the climb (see Appendix B, page 198, for a sample climb map), before removing the holds for later resetting. When the time comes to put the holds back on the wall this map can be consulted as a reference for hold positioning. Try to put as much information on the map as possible to refresh your memory as to which holds go where. This information can include color, manufacturer, size, name of the hold or all of these. If you do not plan on being available to personally reinstall the holds this information is even more critical to avoid confusion and to help insure that the climb is properly reset. You may also want to write numbers on the back of the holds that correspond with number shown on the map. All setters will have to make sure that the T-nuts required to reset the climb are not used for other climbs, or the holds for those climbs will have to be removed in order to reset your climb. With this and all other methods where the holds will be removed from the wall the holds should be kept together (with their mounting bolts to speed up the resetting) in a box so that the eventual re-setter will have the whole climb together and separate from other holds. A good way to mark t-nut used for your climb (and to prevent it from being used for other climbs) is to insert a small foam rubber ear plug (available from home improvement stores) into the t-nut. Simply squeeze and roll the ear plug between your fingers (to compress its diameter) and insert into the t-nut. It will expand back to its normal size within a few seconds. Insert the narrow end into the t-nut and try to keep the outer end almost flush with the wall surface (just leave enough to grab later when removing it). You can also write a number or other reference identifier on the outer end of the ear plug with a permanent marker to speed things up later.

Another method is to take a digital photo of the wall section prior to removing the holds from the wall. All holds should be marked with alignment marks as mentioned above. This can get tricky and still involves a fair amount of labor in installing, removing and then re-installing each hold, and care must be made to not reuse a given T-nut for another problem unless you are planning on sharing the hold already committed to that particular T-nut. If you choose this option, it might be a good idea to mark a few of the T-nuts with a small, labeled piece of tape to use a reference point when re-installing the holds (make sure to also make note of this reference point on the printout of your picture). You would also be wise to take your pictures to reflect more than one climb on a particular section of wall. This not only saves on the total number of pictures that will need to be taken, but also gives you additional points of reference for where holds belong in relation to other holds shown in the picture. Finally print out your picture prior to removing the holds if time allows and write any additional information directly onto the printout.

If you're lucky enough to have enough wall space to have a designated and separate area in which to set your finals climbs, you may be able to obscure the entire area by hanging a tarp or something similar over that wall section. This will allow for a quicker transition time from the open round of your competition (or semi-finals) into the finals themselves by eliminating the resetting time.

## Chalking Holds

When you are done setting your climb, it's best to leave or place a small amount of chalk on the holds. This is done for a couple of reasons. First, if the holds have been newly cleaned they can feel somewhat greasy. While the holds will lose this greasiness after the first few climbers use the hold, you still do not want to give the first climbers the unfair disadvantage of having to deal with a greasy hold. The second reason for doing this is to make the sweet spot of the hold less apparent. Seasoned competition climbers will look at the chalk marks on a hold as much as they will the holds themselves. These chalk marks can help the climber to identify the best portion of the hold to grab (due to the presence of more chalk on this portion of the hold). They can also help identify with which hand the hold should be used (by locating where previous climbers' thumbs have left their chalk mark it's very easy to determine this). When you are chalking the holds, you should not intentionally mislead the climbers by chalking unusable portions of the hold. Rather, you should just chalk the available gripping options with both hands in order to make the correct usage less obvious. Another concern is to make sure that all holds are chalked to the top of the climb. When the proliferation of chalk on holds disappears partway up a climb, it's a pretty good indicator to competitors that others have not made it past this point. It also makes it more apparent to competitors where the crux section is on the climb. By chalking holds all the way to the end of the climb you are helping to instill confidence in the climber that the climb is possible, and also making it less apparent where the true difficulties on the climb lie.

## PUTTING IT ALL TOGETHER

Competition setting sessions can be some of the most enjoyable and most stressful times in which to set. Often you'll be able to work with setters that you don't usually see or set with. As such, it's a great time to pick up on new styles or techniques and to learn from those that might have more experience than you. Enjoy yourself. Do a good job, and know that large numbers of climbers will be coming to the competition with the sole purpose of getting on your climbs and trying to test themselves against them and against the other competitors.

Do your best to make sure that the climbs go the way you want them to. Spend time working with the forerunning crew to fine tune your climbs. Cheat proof (cover over bolt holes and positive hold edges) the holds to limit easier usage options. Finally, hang out for the comp if possible. No one else knows your climbs as well as you do and if there's a question, problem, broken hold needing replacement; whatever – you're the best suited to take care of the situation. Watching a variety of competitors on your climb can be a very instructional experience also, as you can watch climbers of different sizes and with different climbing strengths deciphering your creation. Ask yourself these questions: Did the competitors climb the sequences the way you intended? Were they able to bypass any of your sequences with different beta? Did the holds you selected and used on your climb produce the intended results? Were climbers of different sizes able to do your climb without any height dependency issues? Watching people on your climbs is perhaps the most honest feedback that you can receive on your setting abilities.

Kelly Starke

# COMPETITION CLIMBING ORGANIZATION

By Scott Rennak

There are no set rules when throwing comps, just like there are no set rules to climbing. The key is to plan the right kind of event to accomplish your goals. The following material is how I look at the task of organizing a climbing competition, but it's up to you to sift through these ideas and decide what applies in your situation. I've tried to overview most issues and ask a lot of questions to get you thinking about the options. I'm sure I've missed some things, but I hope this discussion and analysis will help you throw a better comp!

# FIRST THINGS FIRST

Before you start planning any competition, first decide what you want to get out of it. Usually it's a mix of the influences below, but you need to know which is priority #1, #2, etc., so you can make appropriate decisions.

**Build Community:** To give members, customers and area climbers a reason to gather at the gym. If this is your primary goal you always need to remember to keep things fun and social! If folks have fun they walk away with a good impression and they will likely return for the next event (maybe even with a friend or two).

**Market the Gym:** To build awareness of the gym to potential new customers. If this is your primary goal it means you need to spend hours on public relations efforts, calling the local radio, newspaper and TV outlets. There are opportunities everywhere for free exposure, and the unique nature of a climbing competition makes it good material for the media.

**Participate in Ranking:** To be included in a ranking and event hierarchy like USA Climbing's American Bouldering Series (ABS), Sport Climbing Series (SCS) or Collegiate Climbing Series (CCS). If this is your primary goal then you need to pay careful attention to the format, setting, fore-running and judging. Most organizations have strict regulations to follow, so make sure you understand those.

**Re-Set the Gym:** To refresh the gym with new problems and holds. If this is your primary goal it means you'll be spending a lot of time stripping, cleaning and re-setting all the holds. However, many busy gyms recognize the value of an over-haul – members love the new terrain!

# THE FUNDAMENTALS

After you've decided what your goals are it's time to lay out the basic groundwork for the event. Many of the following points are inter-woven and the direction you take with each directly relates to the others.

**Budgeting:** How much money do you have to work with? What are the expected revenues from competitors? What are the expected costs for setting and closing the gym? How much can you spend on promotion? Can you charge for spectators? Can you raise funds through sponsorship? If so, how much? You need to answer all of these questions before planning further. I hear it all the time: "comps always lose money". Well, with proper budgeting they don't have to. I know numerous gyms that turn a direct profit off their competitions (albeit a small one). The biggest expenses for most gyms are lost business from being closed and re-setting costs. Both of these can be minimized, depending on your goals for the event. Hold the comp at the least-busy times (weekdays, nights), keep some walls open for walk-in customers, and don't strip the walls (just set new problems on top). Those decisions alone could literally save you thousands of dollars!

**Scheduling:** The date of any event might be the single most important detail to decide. It must make sense, fitting smartly among other area competitions, local events, school breaks, holidays and seasonal weather. Many well-planned, well-organized events have fallen victim to poor scheduling, and it's always a shame. Minimally call other area gyms to make sure there's no piggy-backing of weekends. It's also good to check regional university calendars, local public school breaks, and look around for other big events in town (not always to avoid them – the success of the annual pro events in Salt Lake City is largely due to scheduling in conjunction with the massive Outdoor Retailer trade show in town). For the average bouldering comp, a Friday or Saturday night is becoming the standard, often you'll only need 3 or 4 hours of main climbing time. This also may allow the gym to stay open for vital weekend business and can provide a wholesome and unique activity on weekend nights. Another schedule option, great for fundraisers, is the day-long "climb-a-thon" where competitors don't need to be there all day, instead dropping in for a shorter session to log their climbs. If you expect a large attendance you may decide it's a good idea to have two separate sessions for adults and youth. Many coaches and youth competitors really appreciate this, and can also allow for slightly different formatting if you are running a sanctioned youth comp but the adult element is not sanctioned. If it's a morning comp be reasonable with the start times, nobody wants to be there at 7am. Be sure to include the full event schedule on the website and flyers.

**Frequency:** How often does this gym hold comps? How often are there comps in this area? If you're dealing with the "monthly-comp" gym or the "weekly-comp" region, you need to be realistic about what attendances will look like. Comp saturation is a reality at times, you've got to keep in mind what the local comp scene is like.

Who's Coming? What's the crowd going to look like? Is this a big weekend event with travelers? Is this a low-key local event where everyone's from nearby? Will it be a spectator-focused event? Are there any special accommodations you should make for large numbers (toilets, garbage, parking) or out-of-town travelers (nearby hotel deals)? How do you market the event properly considering who you're targeting?

**Disciplines:** What kind of climbing comp do you want to throw? Bouldering, roped, difficulty, speed, youth-focused, multi-discipline? Maybe even deep water soloing? Decisions you make here have great impact on the overall nature and cost of the event.

*Tim Kemple*

**Prizes, Raffles and Purses:** There's a great dialog going on about the effects of prizes and raffles on comps. Some gyms and regions wouldn't throw a comp without giving a prize to at least the top 5 in each division. People love it. Other gyms and regions give everything out in a door raffle, and top sponsored climbers couldn't even win anything. People loved that too. Or go for a combination, say a prize to the top 3 overall, top 1 in each division and then put the rest of the booty in the raffle. Door raffles for all competitors are great – who doesn't like to win something? If you feel it's necessary to give the top winners substantial prizes, then maybe you should put together a small cash purse. Many comp winners get prizes that they already have, and they just sell the winnings at bargain-basement prices in the parking lot after the comp. Maybe instead you should give the best booty out in a raffle (or to lower divisions) and give the top dogs cash. If you do they'll thank you for it! Of course some would argue that this whole discussion is crude and competitors should be satisfied with pats-on-the-back. That kind of comp can go over well, but even then there is usually some type of award: shwag, medals, trophies, special t-shirts, sculptures, bronzed-chickens (honestly!) and all sorts of other crazy things. Some comps also give out awards for the most problems, the best costume, the most outrageous chalkbag, and even the worst spandex (not a pretty sight).

**Affiliations:** Do you want to partner with USA Climbing or other comp organization? It means playing strictly by their rules, but you can get a lot of great promotional value for low cost. Plus those organizations have rankings, so affiliation means my competitors earn points which might draw people that wouldn't otherwise have come. In the case of USAC youth events this can often increase attendances dramatically as youth teams tend to travel en masse to comps.

**Benefits:** Do you want to partner with and raise funds for a non-profit, like The Access Fund, the American Alpine Club, Big Brothers and Big Sisters or the local soup kitchen? Maybe there is a popular local climbing organization that could benefit from some funds for re-bolting or trail work. Working with organizations like these can be very fulfilling, can improve attendances and often helps with media coverage and sponsorship fundraising.

**Add-on Events:** Do you want to throw a dyno comp or speed traverse? A slideshow or film screening? Adding events like these can help end the comp with a bang and can even become the highlight of the comp. After-parties have become the norm at many bouldering comps.

# FORMATS, SCORING & JUDGING

Always try to determine the specific format and scoring process early in the planning phase. The first questions you get from competitors are always format-related, so it pays to work out all the kinks well before the comp. Truth be told, it doesn't matter much what specifics you use for the format. The key is to decide everything well before the comp, publish the rules and be consistent in the application of them. It's good when gyms adopt particular rules that apply to the majority of the comps in their region, that way competitors know what to expect. These are the main topics to address, they come up at every comp: REDPOINT VS ONSIGHT VS WORLD CUP

**Redpoint or Onsight:** To begin with, are competitors allowed multiple attempts or just one? If just one, it typically requires an isolation area and strict beta sharing rules to keep the playing field level, like with most high end USA Climbing comps and World Cups. However, most comps use a redpoint format because it's the simplest to manage, more social, and can accommodate more climbers in less time.

**Time Allowed:** Most redpoint comps have a simple 2 to 4 hour period for climbers to complete all their problems. A common onsight format is to allow competitors 5 minutes on each problem separated by 5 minute rests. Whatever time structure you use, be sure it's well communicated and climbers get warnings when their time is running out (tell them "last problem", or "1 minute left").

**Beginning & Ending Attempts:** Typically an attempt officially begins when a climber pulls their weight off the ground (exceptions with jump-start problems). Generally a climber must grab the finish hold and show control of it, some comps ask them to match both hands to make this clear

**Points Earned:** Per send or per hold? That's the basic distinction. Usually it's per send for everyone-climbs-together redpoint comps, and it's per hold for finals and for high-end events. Per send is easier for judging, which can often be left to the competitors themselves (judge each other). Per hold requires dedicated judges that know what they're doing. There are also variations like the World Cup's funky per half-route, or per-hold after a minimum number of moves. For high end comps it's common to break the per hold scoring down even further with small point differences between "controlling", making "useful movement" and touching the "useable surface" of the next hold. Regardless of the system try to make it easy to explain, enforce and calculate.

**Falls:** Do you take off points for falls, record them for tie-breakers, or don't count them at all? Some comps may award 100% of the points for a flash (first-try ascent), 90% for getting it second-go and 80% for any ascent thereafter. You'd make scorecards with all three values printed in columns and competitors would cross off the 100% and 90% after falls (or circle for the send). Another format takes off points for each fall – more falls, more points off. Other places just count the falls but only use it to break point ties (which is essentially the same as taking off a very small number of points, say 1pt per fall when most problems are worth 100+pts). Still other comps don't count falls at all, which simplifies scorekeeping but can yield many ties.

**Final Score:** Most comps these days add up a competitor's top point problems for the final score, usually between 5 and 10. Growing in popularity is the total points method, or total number of problems, although to be effective there need to be at least 60-70 problems. One small detail to be decided: are you adding the top points earned from problems, or the top problems sent? For example, you've counted the top 4 and have to decide on the fifth: a 100pt problem that only earned 80pts after falls, and a 90pt problem that earned 85pts after falls. Which one counts as the fifth? The answer doesn't matter, but you should decide so that it's the same for everyone.

**Divisions:** How many divisions? How do they split? Most comps use the 3- or 4-tier ability system: Recreational, Intermediate, Advanced, Open. These days most comps also have separate divisions for youth, usually breaking down into age categories that match with USA Climbing's divisions. Some comps even have a "team division" to rank the youth teams. Yes, that may mean upwards of 20 divisions! There has to be some kind of difficulty grade associated with each ability division, like up to 5.9 for Recreational, 5.10 for Intermediate, 5.11 for Advanced, 5.12 and above for Open. The specific breaks change from region to region and it's a good idea to be consistent with other events nearby. Obviously there is no way to enforce these ability levels, and every single comp you score will need some "fixing" when the results are first tabulated (see Sandbagging below). The only fool-proof method is to split the entire field into age divisions.

**Sandbagging:** How do you determine if someone is in the wrong division? Sandbagging is almost always unintentional. Some guy in Recreational scored well enough to win Intermediate or place 4th in Advanced. What do you do with that guy? How about the top 3 guys in Intermediate that all would have placed well in Open? It's good to have a policy when facing issues like these.

One popular format makes it easy – there are 10-20 problems set for each ability division and if someone completes 3 problems from the division above theirs they get bumped up into that division. Follow two general guidelines when bumping people into higher divisions – 1) if someone (or a few people) are substantially ahead of everyone else in their division (say 20% above the next people) they get bumped up, or 2) if someone (or a few people) would have placed well in a higher division (say top 10%, or a place that earns a prize) they get bumped up. Sometimes competitors should be bumped up two divisions, but if it's close don't bump them at all.

**The "Gimmie":** You've also got to keep an eye out for the occasional "gimmie" (the accidentally way-over-rated problem) which can skew results, especially if some competitors didn't notice it. For gimmies, it's best is to spread the word early in the comp so that everyone gets the chance to send it.

**Natural Features:** Are they on- or off-route? If a gym has a lot of naturals it's easiest to call them all on (that's how most people climb in gyms). If a gym has few natural features you can go either way. Sometimes they are on for your feet but not for your hands, although that can cause some confusion. The best thing is to call them all on or off, and then clearly mark the exceptions. For exceptions, the setters should put a small sign next to the start: "arête is on/off", "dihedral is on/off", "pebbles are on/off". You may ask setters to mark sections that are off-route with a big red boundary.

**Youth Footholds:** Sometimes youth divisions are allowed to use any footholds to reduce height dependency, although it's ideal for route setters to set for competitors of any height.

**Off-Route:** If a competitor uses a hold or feature that is off-route, what happens? If using the hold helped them significantly the answer is almost always to call them down and score them at the last handhold they controlled before going off-route (or record the fall if it's per send scoring). Conversely, if they just accidentally tap it and it does not help them the answer is usually to let them keep going. The grey area is when it's questionable. In a high-end comp it's best to err on the side of strictness and call them off. For more low-key comps let them continue as long as it didn't really help them. This is a judgment call, so the most important thing is to be consistent with all competitors.

**Cheating:** It might be as blatant as claiming an ascent that didn't happen, or as simple as weighting a foothold that wasn't marked. Regardless, when noticed it cannot be allowed. Be firm but tactful - they might be cheating, but they're also your customer.

**Technicals:** A technical is any instance where the wall, it's fixtures or the belayers or spotters impede the progress of the climber by no fault of the climber. For instance, what if a hold spins or breaks, tape comes off the wall, or the belay is too tight? If that happens often the competitor gets to make the call: if they keep climbing it's ignored and the problem gets fixed when the climber comes down, but if they jump off and call "technical" the attempt will not count against them. It gets extremely tricky during timed finals – typically the climber gets pulled out of the rotation, the problem gets fixed, and the climber comes back out at the end and gets and appropriate amount of time (give them the time that was left on the clock plus some additional time for readjustment). Because of this is highly recommended to use set screws or back-up holds to prevent spinners in any high-end comp – manipulating the running order and climbing times like this always throws an unwelcome kink in the event flow.

**Dyno Comps:** Post-comp dyno events are easy to set and fun to watch, which certainly contributes to their rising popularity. Two general formats are common: a rotation of climbers (one attempt, then back of the rotation, after 2 or 3 falls they are eliminated) or a structured time period (2 or 3 minutes for attempts, then a rest, then another period for attempts, etc.). The rotation is better for spectators (it's action-packed and the best dynoists are left chucking at the end) but it can be hard to distinguish who is 2nd, 3rd, and on. Hybrid formats have worked well too so don't be afraid to experiment. In any case competitors usually cannot complete the same dyno twice.

Margaux Brooke

# SPONSORSHIP

Sponsorships develop relationships with partner businesses to mutual benefit. When writing a sponsorship proposal start by telling them what benefit they'll get out of it. They know what you want, so take the time to tell them what you can give them in return. The standard practice for comps has been to blast out an email or letter to every potential industry sponsor, but times are changing. The poor companies of our little sport get flooded with hundreds, even thousands of requests. We need to be realistic and understand that sponsors must make choices because they can't sponsor everything. Obviously being a customer of the potential sponsor helps a lot, but some businesses are becoming even more selective. With so many options and such limited budgets they need to see bang-for-the-buck. ALWAYS REMEMBER: Businesses sponsor events for the promotional value they receive from that event. If you can provide that value, and show them you did, the sponsor will likely stay involved in future events. And that's what it's all about. It's not about "scoring tons of shwag to give out". It's about having beneficial long-term relationships.

All that said, here are some tips regarding sponsorship:

**Step To It:** Good sponsorship drives are early sponsorship drives. As soon as the ball is rolling I get in touch with key sponsors and affiliates. The whole process can easily take several months and you don't want to rush it.

**Look Local:** The best relationships are local. These are the businesses in the surrounding areas that could turn into customer-generating sponsors. Try to swap with them – some of mine for some of yours. Give them a few free passes to the gym in exchange for sponsorship and you might just gain a new member (who might just book a birthday party or other event). Reach out to the parents of your youth team, their employers may love to support local events and organizations (think banks and real estate and insurance agents). Perhaps businesses you already patronize will get involved like soda or energy bar companies, or even your HVAC or cleaning company. How about local restaurants and brewpubs, or nearly masseuses or yoga studios? Your members probably visit them before or after climbing at your gym, they may already know about you. There are almost endless opportunities for local sponsorship, use your imagination.

**Create Unique Value:** Help your sponsors reach their potential customers, who are your competitors and spectators. Step past logo space and offer tables at the events for demos, sampling and vending, or competitor goodie bags that include coupons or samples. Incorporate them into specific problems or special events. Conspicuous banner and sticker placement can add a lot. Label an entire problem with a sponsor's stickers – it becomes "The Pepsi Problem". Toss out coupons, stickers, samples and even shwag to the crowd (especially during big spectator events). Make sure the announcer talks up the sponsors, not just mentioning their name but talking about their products, business and maybe even their sponsored athletes (who may be in attendance). Display the comp shwag in the gym the weeks before the event to show-off the sponsors and encourage attendance. After the comp create a video with not only sponsor logos, but product placement during the event (maybe a closeup of a sponsor's shoe on a competitor's foot mid-climb, or someone drinking an energy beverage).

**Use Social Media:** Leading up to the event be sure to highlight your top sponsors, share images of the products they're giving away, and talk about how great their company is. Tag them and in turn ask them to share details about the comp on their social media profiles. In today's world this is one of the most visible ways you can promote your relationship with them, and has become a very important aspect of sponsorship.

**Logo Space:** While many organizers think this is key, the truth is logo space has limited value, hence the discussions above. However, you still need to include logos on promotional items like webpages, social media events, posters, t-shirts, postcards, websites, videos, scorecards and more. What normally transpires is the "logo salad" – a mess of sometimes 20 or 30 logos splattered all over the flyer or t-shirt. While you may not have much choice, try to divide the sponsors into levels, each with requisite logo space. Big sponsors get large, prominent logos at the top, smaller sponsors get smaller logos at the bottom and there are slightly limited numbers of each. Keep in mind that more logos means less relative value for each logo. Be sure your top sponsor isn't lost in the mix, put their logo and their banner in the most prominent locations.

## PROMOTION

Effective promotion and publicity can make or break a comp. Every comp will see a higher turnout and better media coverage with effective promotion.

There are two basic goals for promotion:

**Building Attendance:** The only way to have a good attendance is to get in touch with the area climbers. Create an event page on your website, or using a social media service, and share it widely. Send posters to area gyms and shops, post details on social media and popular website message boards, contact local climbing organizations, get listed on community event calendars and anything else you can find to get the word out. Is one of your members or staff super popular online? Ask them to mention the event to their followers, maybe twice! In any postings or flyers always list the essentials like where, when, how much, who's "invited" and basic format details, this can reduce the calls to your gym with questions. You may find it worthwhile to connect directly with the major local youth climbing teams to coordinate with their coaches about registration forms and liability waivers in advance. All that said, probably the single best way to ensure a good turnout is to effectively reach your own customers and members through social media, emails and flyers in the gym. Notify your gym staff well ahead of time and ask them to mention it to customers and members for several weeks prior. Your staff can promote the event, in a personal way, to many, many people. Of course, the best long-term way to build attendances is to throw fun and well-organized comps. If folks have a good time they will return.

**Marketing the Gym:** When handled right a gym can get lots of valuable publicity by holding a climbing comp. It's an opportunity to promote the facility and programming to non-climbers. Send press releases to area TV and radio stations, newspapers, magazines and other community periodicals. Climbing comps are such interesting community stories that most media sources will at least list the comp on their event calendar. Follow-up calls and building relationships with reporters can yield articles and photos, which in turn can yield new customers. Double down on this effort if you are holding a fund raiser or benefit for some local organization, a decent press release and follow up should net you some good coverage.

## THE HELP

Nobody can run a comp by themselves. It takes people setting, handling registration, judging, tallying scores, announcing and much more. With so many parts working together you need to create at least basic (or complex) job descriptions for the staff and volunteers. Days before the comp meet with the various people and groups to explain the responsibilities and answer questions. Do a dry run through all the key processes before show time. Here are brief descriptions of most positions:

**Organizer:** The Organizer calls all the shots and is responsible for running the entire event. However, if you do the job right and train the other staff and volunteers well, there might not be much to do during the event. The Organizer should spend the comp checking with and supporting the other staff, talking with competitors, spectators and sponsors, and putting out the inevitable little fires that pop up. Any Organizer must keep his/her cool when things get crazy and must treat all competitors fairly.

**Head Judge:** The Head Judge trains the other judges, interprets the rules and is the only person who can over-turn a judging decision. Obviously that means the Head Judge must know the rules intimately. Often the Head Judge is also the Organizer or Head Setter.

**Judges:** If you need to use judges try to make sure that they're all people with strong personalities and good judgment. Hold a meeting before the comp to go over the expectations and detailed rules (this can easily take 30-60 minutes). Probably most important is to tell them to be consistent with judging decisions. It matters less what they deem "control" and more that they apply it consistently to all competitors. They also need to stick to their guns when it comes to protests – a waffling judge can cause a real nightmare. If there's an appeal ask the Head Judge to come over and make the call. Provide judges with a clipboard, pen and a complete list of rules in addition to any scoring sheets. For redpoint events make sure to have plenty of judges – nothing can slow down a comp like too few judges.

**Head Setter:** The Head Setter orchestrates the setters and setting and is responsible for the style and grade of the problems. With the help of the fore-runners and other setters, the Head Setter makes all the final decisions regarding holds, moves and problems. The Head Setter should be present for the entire competition to answer questions, fix problems and help as needed.

**Setters:** It's best to have a wide variety of setters to ensure a wide variety of problems. Tall, short, powerful, technical – if the comp is going to be fair it needs variety. The setting and fore-running team should be prepared to spend long hours the night(s) before.

**Fore-runners:** Fore-runners are crucial for any comp. They should be physically fit, have lots of climbing experience, and should be able to analyze movements from the perspective of other climbers. Admittedly it's difficult to be tall and think short, or to have small fingers and project yourself into fat digits. However, it's not the fore-runner who changes the holds or moves. The fore-runner's job is simply to describe "what it's like" to climb the route, and to point out improvements or potential problems. Ultimately the setters or Head Setter make any changes.

**Spotters and Belayers:** Make sure they're experienced, capable and know what the rules are. They could be all you have between yourself and a lawsuit.

**Announcer:** The announcer is the person who keeps the pace of the event moving. For smaller events this may be the Organizer, Head Setter or Head Judge – the pre-comp talk, announcements during the event and the awards and raffle at the end. But for larger events, especially if there will be finals, it's good to have a person dedicated to keeping the energy up the whole time. Meet with the announcer before the event to explain the format and provide them with a list of sponsors (names, products, slogans) and competitor details (names, ages, hometowns, favorite climbing areas). Also try to load them up with "toss-outs" – shwag to throw to the crowd, which is a surefire way to get the audience screaming. The person on the mike needs to be able to excite the crowd while introducing the competitors and explaining the format, all in layman terms without swearing. Some people argue that announcing is the single most important element for a professional-level spectator comp.

**Volunteers:** To ensure a sufficient pool of volunteers post a sign-up flyer and promote on social media a few weeks before the comp (with places for email and phone # so you can contact them). Isolate the specific shifts when you need help and sign-up volunteers for those specific times. Volunteers always respond better when they get something for the experience – passes to the gym, a t-shirt or other shwag. Always try to keep them all hydrated and fed.

**Isolation Monitors:** Onsight format comps typically need an isolation area, and the monitors maintain the integrity of the area. Monitors make sure competitors stay in isolation and watch that they don't communicate inappropriately with anyone outside of isolation. Isolation monitors will escort climbers to the first problem, and will accompany folks to the bathroom. You will need a few, it's practically impossible for one person to hold this position down.

**Desk Staff:** Keep someone at the front desk at all times. For big comps it may require a few people. Unless the comp is a small super-low-key event, it's very unprofessional to leave the front counter un-manned during a comp.

**Photographers & Videographers:** Comps can be the background for great promo photos for your gym, so be sure someone is capturing the moment. Put together a brief comp video complete with bumping music and sponsor props, a great way to add value and keep the hype going well after the comp is over.

# SETTING CONSIDERATIONS

There are countless setting-specific considerations that have a major impact on the quality of a comp. The majority of this book provides an excellent discussion of the concepts by Louie Anderson and other setters. To augment his material, I've included the following list of points to consider:

**Problem Density, Distribution & Variety:** These have an enormous effect on the flow of the comp and the cost of the setting and fore-running. Good density maximizes the number of people able to climb simultaneously while minimizing competitor crashes. Avoid big traverses unless isolated from the problems that go upwards. Best to split the wall into sections, then keep problems from crossing the section boundaries, otherwise it's easy to end up with tons of crisscrossing problems. Be aware of where competitors will be standing, and avoid setting problems over those areas. Watch out for running starts and huge dynos, they need plenty of launching and landing room. Good variety helps ensure everyone has fun, and the playing field is level. Make sure you have some of everything: easy, medium, hard, power, endurance, power-endurance, obvious, devious, static, dynamic, smooth, awkward, underclings, gastons, side pulls, slopers, crimps, pockets, pinches, hard slabs, easy overhangs, mantles, dynos, sit-starts, jump-starts, one-move-wonders and enduro-fests.

**Comps with Kids:** This is probably the single most argued about topic at comps, and with the proliferation of youth teams you better keep kids in mind with your setting. We've all seen it: the irate parent screaming at setters or staff because of a long reach or low foothold. Fortunately there are a few basic tricks that can maximize the kid-friendliness of any problem. First, in the format allow youth divisions to use any footholds (and put extra un-marked footholds in key spots). This won't help short adults, but it does keep the PTA-parents off your back. Second, try to use footholds that can double as small handholds (thus providing some intermediates). Third, avoid super-long reaches. Is it really necessary? Will a small intermediate hold totally ruin the problem? If you must have a big reach make sure the problem isn't graded such that it will decide the winner. Be fair.

**Natural Features:** Natural features can have a major effect on some problems. So, before any wrenches get turned you need to decide if natural features are all "on" or all "off" unless marked otherwise. If there are exceptions, note them at the start of the problem and next to the feature on the wall.

**Labeling:** Clear labeling and a good scorecard are the most effective means of helping competitors navigate their way through the comp. Each problem should have at least the problem # and its point value. You can also dress it up with sponsor logos and the name of the setter. Any special instructions should be clearly marked (any footholds, arête is off, jump start).

**Downclimbs:** Down climbs are safety precautions that help preserve your competitor's bodies. When was the last time a buddy of yours was on crutches after a big fall? Cut us all some slack – put up some big holds for down climbs and bail-outs, especially on high-balls.

**Fall Zones:** Monitor crowded areas, keep everyone back from the walls and keep landing areas free of obstacles (chairs, people, stick-brushes). For finals and high-end comps tape or hang a boundary for spectators. If it's really going to get crazy, issue passes to judges, media and staff to keep everyone else out of important areas.

*Natalia Boltukhova*

**Emergency Kit:** Holds spin and break, and during comps setters need to be ready to fix problems quickly. Before putting away all of the setting supplies pack an emergency setting kit: wrenches, a drill, extra labeling materials (tape), a few generic spare holds (pinch, crimp, pocket, jug, foot chip). Also keep a ladder handy throughout the comp.

**Comp Fore-Running:** One thing to remember is the importance of fresh, in-shape fore-runners. Setters are normally fried by the end of the setting session. Do them a favor and bring in fresh climbers to fore-run. For the typical redpoint bouldering comp, there are two good methods for fore-running and grading the problems: 1) Put a piece of tape or paper at the start of each problem and, after a person completes it, they write their proposed grade on the tape (afterward go around and assign consensus grades), or 2) form everyone into groups and give them each a range of problems to grade (maybe three groups for easy, medium and hard problems). Give problems a slightly higher grade if they're especially long or committing.

**Dealing with Finals:** Special care goes into creating finals and onsight problems. In most cases finals are held the same day as qualifiers with a one- to several-hour break for re-setting. Thus the finals need to be pre-set, mapped and hidden from competitors until finalists are in isolation. The three basic ways to hide finals are: 1) map, mark and strip all of the holds and store in a box for re-setting, 2) map, mark and spin holds and add other holds to camouflage the problem, or 3) leave the holds in place and hang a tarp obscuring the whole problem. In addition to being pre-set, finals problems need to be located wisely. Try to maximize spectator viewing – the last problems should be right in a main part of the gym where everyone can see. Because technicals in finals are such a pain, it's best to make sure any potential spinners have set screws or back-up holds. It's also important for the announcers to refrain from speaking directly about the holds, movement and competitor progress, since this can often be heard in the isolation area and can create unfair situations. For scoring, usually the Head Setter assigns each handhold value. There are many opinions about scoring, but it's less subjective when all finals problems are worth the same points and each hand movement is worth the total point value divided evenly by the total number of hand movements (e.g., a 10-move, 1000pt problem is 100pts per move). A necessary match usually counts as two moves. Falls and flashes earn deductions and bonuses respectively. A popular method is 1000pt problems, 50pt flash bonus and 1pt off per fall (falls are only counted up to the first instance of the highpoint).

*Tim Kemple*

**Isolation Areas:** For onsight formats a competitor warm-up and isolation area needs to be maintained. It's best to have an area with a small warm-up wall, hang/campus-board, some weights, a bike or treadmill or other such equipment. Numerous people should be able to warm-up at the same time. The area should be blocked from view of the competition area (both the climbing and the spectators). The whole idea is that competitors remain isolated from any knowledge of the problems or the performances of other athletes. There should always be at least three staff as isolation monitors (including at least one guy and one gal) so that they can escort competitors to the bathroom (which will always occur, and often).

**Dyno Comps:** A dyno comp can be very complex, with crazy problems spread all over the gym. Or it can be a focused affair on one wall. The quick-n-easy way to throw a dyno comp: put up 4-6 starts (launches) and label them with numbers (#1 to #5), then put up 5-10 finishes (landings) and label them with letters. If you did it right you now have (4-6) x (5-10) = 20-60 dynos! Leave out the variations that are redundant or impossible.

# THE EVENT ITSELF

Most of the organization has been covered up to this point. If your staff and format work properly there isn't much else to do. Yeah, right! Here are some more things to consider before comp day:

**The Schedule:** Work hard to stay on-schedule – it keeps the flow going and adds to the professionalism. Keep things moving, especially at the end when everyone's tired.

**Registration Areas:** Registration staff should be trained and plentiful to help move competitors quickly through. The staff should be able to answer basic rules questions and should have the complete rules on-hand. Before registration opens always check the sign-up station to make sure everything is stocked-up: registration forms, liability waivers, scorecards, pens/pencils, plenty of change for large bills and maybe the t-shirts and registration packs. Someone almost always shows up after the comp starts, so keep registration open.

**Scorecards:** A clear, concise scorecard can be a useful resource and is a sure way to minimize competitor questions about location and grades of problems. Obviously you need to include spots for name, gender, division and a place to list and tally scores. It's also nice to list all of the problems, their points and tape color and include spots to record falls and for judge or witness initials. Add a brief description of the format, a short feedback survey, a map of problems in the gym, a list of setters and a bunch of sponsor logos and you've got a top-notch scorecard!

**Announcing:** Timely, energetic and intelligent announcing sets the stage for a great competition. The pre-comp talk is a chance to kick everything off with a bang. Have a list of things to mention (format, schedule, emergency exits, etc.), crank through the list and get everyone off climbing as quickly as possible. During the comp make regular announcements recognizing sponsors and reminding the crowd about other stuff (raffle, dyno comp, party). At the end, keep the momentum and move fast through the raffles and award ceremonies. If you're going to throw a big event, dyno comp or finals it's nice to have someone dedicated to announcing.

Trevor Harris

**DJs and Music:** Some folks hate it, but thumping beats is the rule of thumb for today's bouldering comps. While not necessary it does keep everything moving and bumping. Whatever music you put on, make sure it's high energy and has a good beat. Many gyms like to have live DJs mixing during and after the comp!

**Livestreaming and Video:** Livestreaming video feeds is a terrific new way to share high end comps. It may require some cost in the form of equipment and personnel, but can add a lot to sponsor value by dramatically expanding your spectator audience. Good commentating is vital since viewers from home have no context except what they see through the screen. It can also be nice to display the video on large screens at the event itself, a great way for audience members to see more of the action than is possible with their naked eye. One of the best parts of a good quality livestream is that you can record it and post it online for people to come back and watch over and over at their leisure.

**Results Tabulation, Posting & Appeals:** Results should always be posted as quickly as possible, but take your time to avoid mistakes. It's a good idea to plan something to fill the competitor's time while you're handling results, so provide something like beer and pizza, a dyno comp, a raffle or slideshow. Results should be tabulated in a separate room or area away from competitors. Prepare the system beforehand and instruct everyone that will be helping. Before going public with results always look them over carefully and see that they make sense (see Sandbagging a few pages back). Once you feel they're ready, print them to hang up in the gym and also post to your event website. Realize that it's very likely there will be a dispute or appeal after the results are initially posted, so be ready to deal with that quickly especially if you have finals. The initial results can always be termed "tentative", with the "final" results posted even days later. Probably the most important factor to producing results quickly is having plenty of calculators and people adding scores. Computers are great for inputting final scores and sorting divisions, but the time-consuming job of adding scores may still be best handled manually. Either way you get data-entry errors, but you can process more scores quicker by splitting the tabulation into two steps: 1) scorecards added by hand by a bunch of people with calculators, and then 2) one person inputs the totals into the computer for sorting. Results for comps with 150+ competitors have been completely processed in under half hour by using a split manual and computer system like this. Double-check the math on each card (ask competitors to add up their score first then you only need to add it once) and double-check that the score is entered into the computer correctly.

**Post-Comp:** Shortly after the event post the final result to the event website and your social media, along with photos and a short description of how it went. You may also want to send it off to the media. Send results and photos to sponsors along with a nice thank-you note (a nice touch is to send them a photo with their own logo or other presence in the image). Also gather important demographic information from registration forms. Many sponsors want to know what the field "looked like" before they signup to sponsor the next event. If you make a video, get it done quick and share it far and wide.

## BOULDERING RISK MANAGEMENT

All gyms have their own insurance regulations and policies concerning risk management, but there is little true advice concerning bouldering and bouldering walls. Bouldering is inherently more dangerous than roped climbing for one simple fact – every fall is a ground fall. Ankles get twisted or broken, heels get bruised and just about anything else can happen in those five to fifteen feet to the ground. However, there are plenty of things any gym can do to improve safety and reduce injuries:

**Set easy down climbs** for boulder problems. Very few comps do this but it's so nice for competitors. For youth especially, jump-offs can be a long drop. Any fall has potential for injury – give competitors a the option to down climb or bail off their problem instead of being forced to jump.

**Watch the crowding.** So many bouldering areas are caves and I've seen some crazy crashes in those confined spaces. If you have a tight cave area keep a close eye on how near the crowd is to the climbing. Standing too close can easily mean getting kicked in the face. And to avoid any potential fire code violations it's good to know the legal limit to the number of people inside the gym.

**Enforce good spotting.** Just like belaying, spotting is a skill, one which most climbers don't understand well. Provide instruction or demonstration before your event in proper spotting techniques.

**Bouldering areas should not be too high.** This is left ambiguous deliberately since different types of padding lend themselves to different height walls. Just remember that climbers often fall off the last moves of a problem. Please keep most of the problems below a reasonable height.

**Bouldering areas should be well padded.** As rudimentary as this statement seems, many gyms don't provide sufficient padding to reasonably prevent injury. Obviously, a climber should be able to safely fall off the top of every problem. If you need it, on the flyer ask that competitors bring crash pads – many will!

*Dan Brayack*

**Bouldering areas should be free of obstacles** such as railings, benches or other hard objects. Climbers can shoot off the wall in any number of unexpected ways, so there shouldn't be any chance of landing on something or hitting something during the fall. If unavoidable, make sure that these items are clearly marked and padded. Also make sure that competitors and spotters (you may want to have extras on hand) are aware of them.

**Qualified medical personnel should be present** for the duration of the competition. Accidents do happen, especially in large groups of people pushing each other hard. Having a well-stocked first aid kit and someone who knows how to use it will pay off if an accident happens. It's also good to maintain an emergency vehicle lane through the parking lot to the gym entrance.

# Scott Rennak

In 1997 Scott Rennak bought a struggling climbing gym. Since then he's been sucked deep into the womb of artificial climbing. Scott has traveled across the country helping gyms throw great climbing comps, and has set routes at over 45 gyms nationwide. He also was a screw-on hold pioneer, creator of now defunct yet once award-winning Crater Holds. Scott was the original founder of the American Bouldering Series, organized the climbing component of the Vail Mountain Games for several years, and has created and staffed many national-level climbing competitions. His views on competition organization and setting developed from working with hundreds of competitions and gyms. These days Scott has settled down in Longmont, Colorado, with his wife and two children.

Tim Kemple

# STYLES OF CLIMBS

## Initial Decisions:

Given the different terrain angles, the assortment of holds available and the movement options at your disposal, the styles of climbing you can set are almost endless. You would be wise though to make some decisions regarding your climb prior to beginning. These decisions will help to narrow the options for lesser decisions during the setting process. These initial decisions include energy expenditure and a choice between replication versus creation.

## Energy Expenditure:

There are basically three different choices here:

**Power** - A climb whose focus is based on extremely powerful movement will usually have a distinctly hard crux that only lasts for a few individual moves, or will be relatively short (1-6 moves) with each individual move having a high intensity level (requiring a 85-100% effort). The focus here is usually on explosive dynamic movement and high muscle recruitment.

**Stamina (aka Power Endurance or Resistance)** – A stamina climb is generally longer than a power climb or will have a longer lasting crux section (6-12 moves) where the moves are still fairly intense but not to the point that they require a climber's maximum effort. Success will usually require a 60 to 85% effort and will usually require the climber to do some fairly challenging moves while pumped.

**Endurance** – This type of climb makes up the majority of the indoor climbs you will find. The entire climb has about the same intensity level with the challenge being overall muscle endurance. The effort required to succeed is usually fairly low (comparatively) and often times it's difficult to pinpoint a specific move or sequence as being that much harder than the rest. The climber will usually feel a slow deep pump and keeping this pump at bay is often the true test of the climb.

## Replication versus Creation:

The basic question here is whether you are trying to replicate a climb, sequence or move that you have experienced elsewhere (indoors or out), or whether you are starting from scratch and attempting to create an entirely new climb. Regardless of which of these you choose every climb you ever set will be one or the other.

**Replication** – The real world offers countless varieties when it comes to climbing. Each type of rock and angle of climbing has its own characteristics that are unique to that style. A setter that climbs outdoors regularly can find no better source for inspiration when preparing to set a climb. Whether you have a specific move in mind or an entire route, often times this other climb is the catalyst for what you intend to set.

Many good setters will routinely travel to different outdoor areas to sample the different styles of climbing to be found and to add new moves and sequences to their bag of tricks. If you haven't had the opportunity to experience different rock types and styles of climbing, you should make the effort to. It will open your eyes to entirely different options than those you might now build into your climbs. These new options will ensure that your setting enjoys the variety that we should all strive for.

If you don't climb outdoors much, or don't have the luxury of traveling to multiple areas and experiencing different rock types, similar exposure can come from visiting different gyms. The differences in wall terrain alone makes climbing in those facilities a learning experience, but also the exposure to other setting styles and hold collections may enlighten you to new ways of setting and different types of movement to offer in your own setting.

Margaux Brooke

**Creation** – Sometimes referred to as "climbing choreography." At its purest form there are only a handful of movement types, each with their own limited number of variations. The way in which a setter combines these moves and the order in which they are encountered on a variety of different hold types provide the individual character of a climb.

Some of the best climbs set this way are made up as they are set, with only a loose idea of what the final result might be. Sometimes the setter will be looking through a pile of random holds when he/she will find that one perfect hold; the one that inspires the vision of the climb to be. Other times a setter will grab a number of holds somewhat randomly and challenge his/her skills to make a climb out of only the options these holds offer.

## SECONDARY DECISIONS:

Once you have made your initial decisions you can further identify the style of your climb by choosing whether your climb will be straightforward or technical, and whether the focus will be on static or dynamic movement.

**Straightforward** – Pretty self-explanatory, this style of climb is fairly obvious and easy to read. The difficulty will usually be a result of difficult to use or small holds, or an accumulation of pump or difficulty. The challenge is not deciding what needs to be done, but in simply doing it.

**Technical** – The movements on this type of climb will be a little harder to figure out, with subtle nuances and often creative use of body positioning necessary to succeed. The climber will need to have good route-finding and sequencing skills and be able to sometimes think several moves ahead of his/her current position on the climb.

**Static** – A static climb is one in which the climber will be in control throughout the entire climb, transitioning from one sequence to another with fluid and precise movements. The climber will usually maintain three points of contact with the wall and will be able to recover from any misread sequences or reverse failed movements. The overall challenge will be to complete the sequence or climb in its entirety, rather than risk a low percentage singular move or sequence of moves.

**Dynamic** – There are two types of dynamic movement; the deadpoint and the dyno. In both types the movement from handhold to handhold is done with a much faster, more dynamic movement, often with a higher risk of failure and usually by way of moves that are much more difficult to recover from and reverse if failed. During a deadpoint move one or both feet will stay connected to their footholds or the wall. On a dyno move the feet will lose contact and more force will be transferred to the target hand hold(s). The difficulty of dynamic movements can be generated from a long movement, moving to or from a bad hold or set of holds, or by trying to generate the movement from an awkward position.

## Other Options:

**Campusing** – The term campus refers to movement begun from a hanging position where neither feet have contact with the wall or holds. Originally used as a training method to increase muscle recruitment and dynamic precision strengths, it can also be implemented into setting on steeper terrain where a section of wall is to be crossed using a minimum of holds (usually with more positive holds than when supplying footholds on the same terrain). Sections of campus climbing can be used for vertical gain, to cross roofs, arches or bulges, and for short traversing sections.

**Leaning or Traversing** – Leaning lines are obvious choices when following lips or diagonal roof systems. They will often involve a lot of tracking and will usually present many options for heel and toe hooking. Traversing lines may share many of the same characteristics as leaning lines, with the addition of several matching (hands and feet) options and crossovers or crossthroughs.

**Drop Downs** – Often used on shorter height walls, these types of climbs will have the climber move upward (and often slightly diagonally in one direction or the other) before reaching a point in the climb that requires them to lose elevation before again moving upward. This "drop down" can be made by actually down climbing, or moving dynamically by actually dropping or dynoing to the next lower hold(s).

**Theme Setting** – Often times it is nice to set with a theme. This theme can either be implemented using a similar hold type throughout the climb, or by repeating a similar movement pattern. Theme setting can be a great tool to expose and target specific weaknesses or strengths of a given climber or group of climbers. Good examples would be climbs where the majority of the holds are slopers, or perhaps a climb that is filled with underclings.

## Specific Considerations:

Each of the different disciplines of indoor climbing (bouldering, toproping and leading) present their own unique considerations and benefits. Depending on the discipline in which your climb belongs, please keep these in mind.

## Bouldering

Every fall is a ground fall. Be aware of landing areas and fall trajectory. Every effort should be made to prevent awkward falling positions or a fall trajectory that would send the falling climber into a fixed object or other obstacle.

Depending on the height of the wall and the available floor padding it may not be wise to position the most difficult moves or low-percentage dynamic moves, high on the problem.

Climbers will usually be able to see the entire problem from the ground. Due to this feel free to mix things up and try to create difficult to read sequences.

Because of the shorter length of most boulder problems, avoid rests on all but the longest of problems or traverses.

As the only way down in most cases is to either down climb or jump off, position down climbing jugs adjacent to harder problems whenever possible. These can either be random holds set specifically for this purpose or be incorporated into an easier adjacent problem.

## Toproping

Given the security of the rope above, all but the shortest of falls are eliminated from this discipline. As such feel free to incorporate lower percentage moves into your climb.

Because there is no need to provide secure clipping holds, toprope climbs can be considerably more sustained than other roped climbs.

As the rope will generally hang free from the top anchors be especially careful when setting traversing climbs or climbs on steeper terrain. A fall low on the route can send the climber swinging wildly (either laterally or backwards). Make sure that there are no protruding holds or other obstacles that the climber could swing into and that he/she will not swing into walkways or other congregating areas for spectators and other climbers.

## Leading

You will usually want to make sure that at least the first few clips are made from somewhat secure holds or stances. As the climber gets higher on the climb (and further from the ground) you can start to incorporate more challenging clipping options. Always decide in the direction of safety when questioning your clipping choices.

Be aware of the potential fall trajectory of climbers and make every effort to insure that no obstacles, walls or protruding holds will be hit in the event of a fall.

The initial moves of a lead climb (up to the approximate height of the first bolt or so) are often set to incorporate a challenging sequence or "mini-crux." The reason behind this is that the starts to lead climbs are often used as overflow bouldering options within climbing gyms. By setting with this in mind you can greatly enhance the climbing options in your facility.

Due to the ability to wander freely (within reason) lead routes provide great opportunities for variations and link-ups with other adjacent routes. You can often create these other climbing options with the addition of only a handful of additional holds.

*Megan Mascarenas at SCC Colorado Springs, CO - photo Alex Ford*

# Molly Beard

Molly's routesetting career began in 1995. In the past 18 years she has set for more than 20 Nationals or Continental level events and is currently the only woman to hold a USAC L5 certification. She currently works as a freelance routesetter across the US. She lives in Portland, OR with her fabulous husband and 2 water loving cats.

# Women and Routesetting

By Molly Beard

In 1999 I set my first 'big' event: a Regional Championship. I was the only woman on that team, a trend that would continue at all the Championship events I worked on until 2007. In a strange way it was kinda flattering, and appealed to the vanity I wish I didn't have, to be surrounded by guys. In a very real way I do enjoy working with guys: the banter, the bad jokes, the pranks, it is all good for my tomboy heart. Then I got to work with Jackie Hueftle at the 2007 ABS Jr. Nationals. I was psyched!

Why so psyched? What could be so different about working with men or women? We all know men and women climb differently, just as we know adults and kids climb differently. You can quantify it physiologically: differences in muscle mass, center of gravity, height and hand size. You can attempt to quantify it psychologically; but if that is difficult to do with climbing it is doubly difficult to do with setting. I could not deny that being a woman setter makes a difference, but I was unable to articulate those differences until I had another woman to work with!

There are, it turns out, LOTS of differences, and women setters bring quite a bit to the table. The obvious things are size and strength issues: we are relatively smaller and weaker than our male counterparts, making it easier for us to set specifically for women and kids. We are relatively more technically competent, ensuring that a gym's route repertoire is more diverse. We also tend to have more endurance and be better at resting, making it easier for us to identify rests where they may not be wanted.

If women bring so much to routesetting why are there so few of us? I have spent many years thinking about this topic and have come to the conclusion that there are two big misconceptions that women setters are up against 1) women's personalities are problematic and 2) women won't do physically demanding jobs.

One reason the female personality is perceived as problematic is the social norm that women don't or shouldn't like tools. This, of course, is crap. I know few women who don't own, and adore, their cordless drill; I mean really, you've gotta have a way to hang stuff on your walls! Another part is one of how women shouldn't enjoy work that is considered 'manly'. Again, crap! Why shouldn't women enjoy some satisfactory problem solving? The third and less talked about reason is the perception that women don't take criticism well. I'm not sure how many of you have worked with women, but I will argue that women have an equal to greater ability to listen to criticism than men do. There are difficult members of both sexes, just as there are affable ones. In regards to setting, all the personality necessary is an open mind, a willingness to work hard, and knowledge of basic movements and tools. Bulging shoulder muscles are not required.

The perceived physical demands are another reason that women might not be enthusiastic about setting. As an experienced setter I will tell you that yes, routesetting is hard work, and yes, it does demand a working understanding of rigging and aid-climbing, but in reality the job is no harder than a climbing workout, and rope skills are no harder to learn than the basics of leading. With education on the use of ascenders and pulley systems, even the tiniest woman can race up a fixed rope and haul buckets of big holds without getting exhausted.

For so long I had thought of myself as a setter who happened to be a woman. After more than 18 years in the profession I have come to realize that it is not only okay, but *important*, to see myself as a woman setter, because I do offer some different things to gyms and comps than men. I look forward to what the other women setters in the country will accomplish!

# Sandcastles

By Molly Beard

When I first started climbing there were no taped routes. The gym would simply strip all holds from a section of the wall, clean them, and then replace the holds in a random configuration.

The game was to make up problems to try and burn our friends off, and all the climbers did it. Essentially, all of us climbers at the time were routesetters, and we all dealt with the smack-talking and praise for what we created, but only from our immediate circle of friends.

Then the advent of colored tape arrived. I remember thinking how silly it was, as it seemed to me that taped routes took away creativity from us. I mean really, why would I want to follow in someone else's footsteps? In hindsight what we did making up problems was no different than taping them; it just wasn't out there for all to see.

After setting for my first 'comp', well, more of an in-house social event, I truly discovered how rewarding the process of setting and most importantly sharing with all climbers could be. I also learned how hard receiving criticism could be!

No longer insulated by my close pals, I heard earfuls from climbers of all types. "It's too reachy," said the tiny 6 year old. "It's too scrunchy," said the tall guy. "It's too weird," said the gym owner. For everyone and every climber type there was a 'too-much' of something!

My initial reaction was one of arrogance. I could climb my routes just fine, thank you, why couldn't you? My second was despair. I tried so hard, why was no one happy? My third was frustration. Why are these people bitching so much?

This was my first ego bruising, but it wouldn't be my last. After the comp was over I started to think about what had happened, and had a fantastic epiphany. My job as a routesetter was first and foremost to please the customers at my gym. Since I had no real teachers at first, I would have to rely on my customers' feedback to get better. That meant taking all the criticism with a smile and a big dose of humility. Ouch!

Almost immediately I had a second revelation. Routesetting is just like building sandcastles. It goes up, it is enjoyed (or not) by the public, and then it goes away. It will never matter if I just created a Renoir or fifth symphony of routes, it will disappear just as fast as the garbage. So why allow my ego to get in the way?

Ego is a basic, if sometimes unpleasant, part of being human. We will never be able to escape from it. Psychologists tell us over and over: That when you invest yourself into something (work, education, relationships, sport, you name it) you place your ego, and therefore your identity, on the line.

We must drop our egos long enough to listen to what people have to say about what we've done, because listening is the first part of learning, whether from a customer or from a mentor/teacher. Granted, the feedback from a beginning climber might not be as useful as that from an experienced routesetter, but almost all criticism has a little nugget of goodness in it; the hard part is trying to sift it out.

No routesetter can please 100% of the climbers in any gym; there are just too many variables in body sizes, types and strengths. The best we can do is to step up and try to walk that fine line of ego and learning; to care enough to set quality routes, embrace feedback, and therefore get better.

# Motivation

By Matt Bosley

Hello, my name is Matt Bosley. I have been climbing for about eighteen years and route-setting for the past ten. I began setting at Earth Treks Climbing Center, in Maryland. Earth Treks has always valued good route setting, so I was lucky to be able to learn from the talented setters that had come before me.

Throughout the years many people have asked me questions about route setting. There was one question that popped up several times, that wasn't easy to answer at first. What keeps you motivated to set routes every day? I always knew that I loved climbing, but this answer seemed too easy and not thorough enough. To many people setting can be seen as a mundane repetitive task, and some aspects of route setting are. To answer this, I focus on the artistic side of route setting. For me, there are two parts to the setting process the mechanical side and an artistic side. The mechanical side is all of the repetitive parts, which involves fixing lines, stripping routes, washing holds. However the artistic side is the part that seems to have no limits. This is the part that I enjoy, and keeps me challenged.

The artistic side of route setting is not physical. It is an overall plan for a blank wall, how each grip will be turned, and how all of that relates to the overall route. Climbing outdoors, climbing in competitions, and day to day interactions within my own community, give me motivation and fuel the artistic side of my route setting.

Motivation is different for everyone, but all route setters are climbers. So, I would like to start there. My motivation primarily comes from my climbing experiences. The challenge of that is how to translate my experiences onto the wall when I get back into the gym. As route setters, our jobs depend on us constantly coming up with new ideas. For me, I need to climb in different places regularly, to broaden my vocabulary of movement. When I return with my new inspiration, I rarely set specific moves, instead I focus on the general style of the climbing area that I was just at. After I have figured out the logistics of setting that style of movement, I then try to mix it with other styles of climbing that I am more familiar with. Over time these themes accumulate into a vocabulary of movement, which helps me grow as a climber and as a setter.

Outside of my own gym, but still in the plastic realm I gain motivation from attending competitions and climbing at other gyms. Competitions are a great way to see and experience other route setters' best work. I find that competition boulder problems and routes, typically are more creative and thought provoking than routine gym climbs. This is probably due to many reasons, the most common being the extra time and effort put in by the route setters, the availability of more and sometimes new holds, and the blank slate that appears after the entire gym is stripped. I also like competitions because they help me with my hold ordering. When I see and touch a climbing hold in a competition or at another gym, I am more likely to buy that hold. Rather than holds that I have only experienced through a catalog. This is also why I tend to support hold companies that sponsor competitions.

Within my own gym, I am motivated by the things that most setters get psyched on. Holds, holds, holds! They always seem to make routes set themselves. This does not mean that you have to buy new holds, but that doesn't hurt. It could be as simple as stripping two routes on opposite side of the gym and challenging yourself to set the opposite walls with the given holds. Volumes also motivate me. We are fortunate to have many custom made features in our gyms. We have features that resemble everything from a giant canoe to a helicopter and many little ones in between. I feel movable features and volumes are very important to a climbing gyms longevity. By putting a large volume on the wall a setter can completely change the terrain in that area. This keeps everyone more engaged. First, it challenges the setter to set around a new obstacle. Second, it gives the members drastically different routes on walls that they are accustomed to climbing on. In addition, volumes are relatively easy and inexpensive to make, which is an added benefit.

Finally, no gym would be any fun without all of the people who share it. I think that the most important thing that we can do as route setters, is listen to the folks who we set for. Every climbing gym or area has a community and every community is slightly different. However; I feel that climbers everywhere want the same basic things from a gym, to have fun and to grow as climbers. Our challenge as route setters is to figure out what motivates them and use our experience to make new and exciting climbs.

*Caroline Treadway*

# Ward Byrum

To me routesetting is an amazing form of art. The relationship climbers have with our work is what makes routesetting so special to me. People interact with our creations, they interpreted them, try to climb them, and hopefully dream about them. It's a craft that is accessible to anyone with a wall and some holds but yet takes years of dedication to become proficient. I've explored the art of routesetting for the past 17 years. Over that time I've worked with some amazing setters, Chris Danielson, Tonde Katiyo, Mike Pont, to name a few. I feel the art of routesetting is best learned through experimentation, and an openness to new ideas and concepts. At Planet Granite in California I learned the importance of professionalism in routesetting. I feel fortunate to be able to set routes everyday as the head routesetter for Earth Treks in Rockville Maryland.

# Hold Choice

By Ward Byrum

As Routesetters we are presented with a plethora of choices on a daily basis. Where to set, how hard, what to play on our ipods........but I feel hold choice is the most important. This choice goes far beyond basic hold type, it encompasses everything we do as setters. The holds we put on the wall help determine the grade of our routes, how comfortable they are to climb, and what other people perceive as our intended sequences. Before making this choice we must first decide the objective of a move in order to choose a hold that completes that objective the best. Hold choice can turn a potential rest position into a pump inducing crux, or what was a clumpy foot traverse into a delicate smearing foot sequence. The decision to either up or down size your hold selection is the key to setting a sustained and quality route. I am going to present a few scenarios we encounter while setting and attempt to show how thoughtful hold selection can affect the quality of product we create.

## The basics...

There are thousands of holds on the market today, not all, but most are designed to be used in a certain way. Mainly I am referring to right and left handed holds. Correctly identifying and using these holds appropriately is a basic skill every routesetter should possess. Routesetters have argued over this since the dawn of time so I am not going to attempt to define the differences in this essay. In a way it doesn't matter, what matters most is that you think about it. Make a decision and don't use holds out of convenience. Like most things in life it's all but impossible to be lazy and really good at something at the same time. If you're like me you've found yourself four moves from the shuts, with nothing left in your setting bucket but left handed holds a million times. You have a choice; you can use the left handed holds as right hands or go retrieve the holds you really want to use. I haven't always made the extra effort but when I don't, I know I didn't put up the best product I could and that eats at me. There is a certain amount of professionalism we need as routesetters if we want to be taken seriously by gym owners and management. Most people think we just screw holds on a wall and hope it doesn't suck! Let us not prove them right. If you want a climber to use a hold only for his left hand you can encourage this by using a hold that feels and looks like a left handed hold. If you want them to match, use a match hold, if you don't then use something smaller. Giving a climber a clue to your intended sequence should help them climb your route in sequence and in doing so will find the route is easier, flows better, and hits the targeted grade.

## Ouch!

Climbing outside isn't always comfortable. Sometimes a crimp is just so sharp only a masochist would want to pull on it, luckily most climbers are a bit masochistic. As routesetters we have the power to smooth these sharp crimps out, add texture to greasy footholds, and place big comfortable finish holds to clip the shuts from. In short we have the ability to make our climbs better then outside. Through careful hold selection we can make each hold perfect for each intended move. We still need climbing to be hard but using a hold that has too sharp of a lip for the terrain is a good way to ruin an otherwise perfectly good route. Not all jugs are the same, most have a wall angle that they work best on, paying attention to the comfort and ergonomics of your grips will let the climber focus on the movement rather than how much their hands hurt. Using a hold with a sharp incut and a narrow lip on a wall that is not steep enough, it will dig into the climbers hands and cause uncomfortable pressure on the joints. You should want your climbers to enjoy the movements you create not the fact that they got to show off their pain tolerance.

## Make them use those $100 shoes...

I find the biggest difference between climbing outside versus in a gym is the precision required in your footwork. The more we force our gym climbers to use delicate footholds the more easily they will transition to climbing on the real thing. Using the smallest foothold "possible" will require the climber to concentrate on their foot placement. You will also make it harder to switch feet which will add foot sequences to your routes, increasing the subtlety, and intricacy of the movement. It is possible to take this idea too far, so it's important to understand the demographic you are setting for and their limitations. You don't want to sandbag a beginner climber by forcing them to use the worst footholds you have on a 5.6. So before heading up on a rope I like to think about the grade of route I'm setting, the terrain, and possible movement styles I may want to incorporate. Once I've accessed these variables, I then choose a variety of foot holds to take up with me. In general you should size most of these footholds to fit the difficulty your trying to set, then throw in a couple clumpy feet and a few really bad smear feet as well. To use these footholds properly you will first need to decide their purpose. I define footholds as either push or pull feet. If you want a climber to high step to an outside foothold and then pull down on it with their foot, it needs to have a positive edge. The same goes for a smearing foot, if you want them to perform a series of foot sequences in order to obtain a higher perch then you have to make the feet so small that they can't stand hard on one and then high step to the next. A well placed, hard to stand on foot can also add a bit of risk or drama to the movement. A foot hold with a large surface area is easy to switch feet on and takes more pressure off of the arms, so should be used sparingly on hard climbs and generously on easy ones.

## No crux, no recovery.

The basic idea here is sustained movement on consistent holds. When choosing a hold it's critical to understand how incut the hold should be and how changing this effects the movement. Even people with a limited understanding of climbing know that a sloper is harder to hang onto than a positive incut jug, that's just common sense. It's the grey area between these two types of grips that we are concerned with. It is my preference to set routes with either sustained or progressing difficulty. Again trying to make our routes better then outside. This is achieved by eliminating both cruxes and rest positions. I also prefer setting with a maximum number of moves. In general the higher number of sustained moves you can force a climber to do the more of a pump you'll induce. If you make any of the holds on your route too large you'll create an opportunity for the climber to fully recover, therefore erasing the pump you worked so hard to create in the previous moves. Rest holds also create an interruption in the flow of a route. Holds that are too large or too incut will also make it easier for a climber to skip moves and botch sequences. To avoid this you should try and make the hold just positive enough that they can only reach the next hold in the sequence. If a hold is so large that you can pull down and out on it then they can lock it off too far or even generate momentum to jump to the next hold. If you scale the holds down the climber will have to remain under to hold in order to maintain contact, this will make the moves smaller and up the difficulty. This trick is particularly useful when setting for kids. Now if you want them to jump to a hold consider making it a bit larger so they can grab it while flying through the air. Just remember if they can jump to it they can most likely rest on it as well. I usually counter this by placing any feet far outside their center of gravity so they'll have to maintain a tense core while trying to rest and by making the moves after the jug a bit harder. This will help force them back into a pumped state. If you push this concept too far at one particular spot on a route you'll create a definable crux and it will likely cause you to miss your intended grade as well.

## Seduction...

The size of a hold is a great way to get a climber to do what you want, let's be honest, we all love big jugs. If a jug is big enough a climber won't be able to stop themselves for grabbing it, once they have committed, you can easily force the next sequence of moves. You can seduce a climber into using a certain hold that they may be able to skip just by making it a little larger. This concept works particularly well with an undercling. On easier grades a climber will often try everything short of levitation to avoid using an undercling, but you can entice them into it if it's bigger than the other holds around it. On harder routes make sure not to overdo it, making it just slightly larger will go a long way (think, showing them a little leg, not a full on proposition). This technique can work with footholds as well. For example if you want to make a climber dynamically swing their feet from one side of the wall to the other, simply deteriorate the feet on one side and then place a seductively large foot on the other, their survival instincts and common sense will do the rest. Also the larger it is the further away it can be which will make forcing this move easier as well.

# Practice

## Flat Edge Challenge

In this exercise you're asked to pick a wall that has lots of angle changes and attempt to set a route with only flat edges, meaning no incuts or slopers. To complete the objective you'll have to choose holds that create a perfectly flat edge once attached to the wall. For example a hold with a 45 degree incut on a 45 degree wall will make a flat edge. When the wall angle changes, you have to keep adjusting the holds to create that flat edge. It is an easy concept but can be challenging for even veteran routesetters. You should find the route is hard to rest on and is really comfortable to climb.

## Foothold Selection

This exercise deals with footholds. First set a simple boulder problem on a vertical wall, and try to avoid tracking (using handholds for feet), the grade does not matter. Then climb it. Once you have an idea of the movement and difficulty involved try downsizing all of the feet. Climb it again. The concentration required to stay perched on your feet should have been increased, as well as the difficulty. Repeat this exercise until the foot holds are just too bad to use. I think it's important to push this exercise to the point of making the footholds useless. This will give you a better understanding of when to turn up the precision, when to dumb it down, and by how much.

## Handhold Selection

The next exercise is just like the one above but you only adjust the handhold size, or rather how incut the holds are. Try to notice how much shallower your lock off is as you make the hold less incut. The subtlety involved in the movement will increase as well. You will no longer be able to awkwardly lunge to holds but will be forced to climb with precision as your grip becomes more tenuous. Any self-respecting climber can lock a jug off to his shoulder, but past it? What happens when it is not a jug? Even a small adjustment in hold size can make a big change in difficulty and increase in the pump a problem creates. You'll want to take careful notice of how changing holds in this way effects movement and difficulty.

## Summary

With all these choices we have to make as routesetters it's a miracle we ever finish a problem. But with practice the decisions will become second nature. Strategic hold selection will add finesse to your routes and will create a more memorable and intimate experience for the climber. Intimate? When projecting a route outside you remember the minuscule details of the holds, how hard to push on certain feet, when to rest and when to gun it. It is the complexity of this coordinated effort that creates a complete experience. As routesetters we have the power to make our hold choices just as memorable. As your hold choices become more refined you'll be able to make better tweaks to other setters' problems as well as your own. I find adjusting a hold's size is the best way to alter another routesetter's work without causing unnecessary conflict. Not only is it more efficient, but an adjustment in hold size is less prone to objection from the creator. It allows the original intent behind the movement to remain intact; only adjusting the difficulty, risk involved, or comfort of a move. Members of your gym or competitors at your competition are paying good money to climb on your routes. They deserve the best hold choice for each situation not just the next hold at the top of your bucket. The point of all of these choices should not be to make a route hard, but rather to create a route that is as good as it can be and that best completes your objective. If you're trying to set a 5.12, why not make it the most thought provoking, pump inducing, foot concentrating rig in the gym, instead of a 5.11 with one hard move off of a right handed pinch that has been flipped upside down and used with the left hand? Better hold selection is pivotal in the creation of 5 star routes, which flow seamlessly through consistent intuitive movement. At the end of the day it's the combinations of all these decisions that make our routes the very best they can be.

# Chris Danielson

03.15.13

Chris Danielson is one of the most experienced and accomplished competition routesetters in the world, a top professional consultant in the climbing wall industry, and a representative of leading climbing brands. Chris has worked at over 50 major competitions in the US and abroad and been Chief Routesetter of many National competitions. Since 2005, he has worked with USA Climbing in developing the USAC Routesetting Clinic and Certification Program and has instructed dozens of clinics and workshops. He also serves on the Rules Committee of USA Climbing, the Certification Standards Committee of the Climbing Wall Association, and is the only active IFSC certified International Routesetter from North America.

With his company Thread Climbing, LLC, Chris has assisted multiple climbing gyms in business planning, operations, and facility and climbing wall design, including Sender One Climbing, Stone Gardens, and Triangle Rock Club. Chris works as a representative for e-Grips, So iLL, Teknik, and Trango to the climbing wall market in North America, and is a sponsored athlete with Five Ten. He holds a Master's in Social Science from the University of Chicago and attended Miami University of Ohio as an undergraduate. When not working, climbing, or thinking about climbing, Chris may be found watching movies, playing Tetris, and drinking Diet Pepsi.

# "Every Movement is a Lesson"

Chris Danielson

As routesetters we try to imagine and then manifest variations of specific movement that create interesting and enjoyable climbing indoors. At our most inspiring moments, we deliver intriguing new lines that spark relatively fresh sequences that look and climb more excitingly than the average line. Sometimes our routes are climbed by hundreds in a matter of hours in competition, and if we're lucky, seen by hundreds or thousands more spectators at an event or in a video. But most of our efforts are behind the scenes, and a much greater percentage of our work is climbed more often by far less people - our own climbing friends and small communities - at our commercial home gyms, bouldering hangouts, or recreational and fitness walls on which people are often being introduced to climbing for the first time.

As climbers, we perform at our best when we can intuit sequencing and move with fluidity even when challenged intensely. As often as possible, routesetters try to inspire climbers to reach that point while psyched about the movement we create. We want climbers to come back tomorrow to work the moves, send the route, or, if they on-sighted it, to tell their belayer how fun it is and that they should hop on themselves. Yet reaching this goal everyday is hard to maintain, and we often need inspiration ourselves. Needless to say, the grind of everyday setting has put most experienced setters through patches of boredom, creative blocks, and a yearning for insight to something original.

Some setters may just be learning how to select and manipulate holds, turn wrenches, and force movement. Others may have set so many routes that when it comes to naming them, free association works fine. Regardless of experience we all find ourselves creatively blank on occasion, and when we do, it is helpful to remember that although turning a wrench and tightening a hold may sometimes seem simple or redundant, the implications of each choice we make are much more complicated.

## IMAGINE THIS SEQUENCE...

"Right hand crimp on slightly left-turned flat one-pad side-pull Voodoo crimp with left hand down and left four feet, pulling upward on sloping under-cling pocket. Turn head down and step left foot through right on geometric flat horizontal e-Grips edge, while left knee is turned outward and center of gravity is gradually raised over the left foot. Once solid left foot pressure is established, extend right leg out diagonally right and post foot delicately on wall texture until center of gravity is well balanced over left foot. Focus head movement upwards to re-adjust crimp and insure right thumb is wrapped tightly over corner edge of hold. Pull body in towards the wall and slowly raise right leg vertically to sloping Franklin disc foothold. Pull tightly with left hand fingers in pocket against hold texture to maintain body tension. Lock-off right hand crimp by pulling with forearm

and bending elbow out while increasing pressure over right foot and releasing left foot to flag against wall behind right leg. Keep as much body weight as possible over right foothold and raise body vertically through extending right leg and gradually flagging further up and out right with the top of left foot. Hold body tension to release left hand from pocket and reach slightly up and left three feet from right hand crimp to left hand Etch gaston. Turn head down to reach high on gaston and work fingers up into the hold slowly but with sustained power until hold is controlled with left hand."

The detailed paragraph above describes one single left hand movement that incorporates five climbing holds in the progression of a route. Depending on the size of the holds and the degree of wall overhang, the movement described might be 5.9 or 5.13. Regardless of the level of difficulty, for a climber trying at his/her limit, it actually involves more like 25 – 30 distinct body movements.

It may have taken the routesetter five minutes or less to imagine the movement and bolt these holds to the wall, but it may take a climber weeks or months of struggling through the sequence to complete the moves, and eventually the entire route. For beginners, just learning and trusting the body movement above can be a serious challenge, and even for strong and experienced climbers who understand the movement, learning how to do it most efficiently in order to maintain strength, power, and balance to complete the route can be incredibly difficult.

As routesetters, every time we put a hold on the wall there are diverse results. Climbers will love the route. Climbers will hate the route. Climbers will think the moves are reachy. Climbers will think the moves are scrunchy. Climbers will say it was boring, or the crux sequence seemed out of place, or the holds were greasy or the texture was great, or it hurt their fingers, or, rarely - that it flowed with perfection. Climbers will flash or fall, send or get crushed, but among all the various results, one will be that every climber that pulls on that hold, whether they know it or not, is learning something about climbing movement. Beginners learn general techniques like how to trust their feet or high step. Intermediate climbers work on flexibility and understanding the dynamics of drop knees or opposition strength. Elite climbers are often those who are always intent on learning more themselves, and may be focusing on how to unlock intensely difficult single movements. And during a session where a crew is working a project, even the guys in the corner with sneakers on are learning something by watching. Consciously or unconsciously, people are always learning about climbing movement.

Regardless of our experience level, we share our own basic or complex understandings of climbing techniques and styles through a unique endeavor. We sift through piles of holds for just the right grip, tweak the angle of direction to create the movement imagined, and turn a wrench to finish the product. Right now thousands of climbers are learning through movement routesetters created. When we are bored or tapped out or trying to think of something innovative, just remembering that we have the ability to teach someone something about their movement every time the wrench turns can be good motivation.

In addition to improving climbers' abilities, we also have the potential to create strong relationships between climbers and the gyms they climb at, and inspire them to come back the next day to send. The better the relationships we create, the stronger the communities that are built around indoor climbing facilities. And the more we think about building routes as the potential to teach someone something about climbing, the more we can understand as routesetters about climbing in general - how the dynamics of movement work, and how to create new, challenging, and enjoyable sequences. Through remembering that every movement is a lesson, we can keep motivated to create a great product for climbing communities and be inspired to learn more ourselves.



*Caroline Treadway*

# Jacky Godoffe

Born in 1956 near Fontainebleau, began climbing in 1980. 1m79 tall, maybe little less now; 62 kg, have never changed weight in 30 years! Classically trained for piano and guitar - I still play, but not enough! 10 years of gymnastics taught me coordination, but unfortunately not footwork! Professional climber for 2 years, but I prefer having my passion and profession separate. Married with 5 kids. Schoolteacher for 15 years. National trainer and setter for the French Climbing Federation since 1992. Journalist for the French magazine Vertical for 10 years. Photographer and author of many Fontainebleau guidebooks and a kind of autobiography : *"Le joueur de blocs"*. 35 years of mostly bouldering in Font. 20 years of route setting, more comps routes and boulders than I can remember - some awesome and some nightmares. And that's why I keep setting - Doubt is my driving force. My best memory… tomorrow maybe, life is for climbing! A dream: write a book about setting, but it's such a huge job! I'm not in a hurry and I still have a lot more to learn.

# The 5th Element

By Jacky Godoffe

As a tyrannosaurus of climbing and route setting, I have always been focused on a potential *5th element*, that could be added to all the other theoretical ones; basically anything different from usual practice. I don't actually have a clear idea of what it could be most of the time, but if I did I would have lost the psych for this game a long long time ago. Obviously it hasn't happened yet! Because the topic is route setting, I will try to expose my views on the constant search of new dimensions.

## Climbing competitions: child of rock climbing history

Historically, climbing is a very open sport that requires many skills. Small, tall, thin or heavy climbers can find a way to push their own limits. As I see it, one of the best factors of progression is the ability to be endlessly surprised by the playground. That's why on rock, climbers like to change areas to expose themselves to new experimentations. It is inconceivable for me to constrain the competitors required abilities and I always try to create some element of surprise when I set for any comp.

## Limits of the playground

Let's begin with some limits or rules, a personal free adaptation of the four fundamental elements in nature :

**WATER** there are clear rules we need to play with as route setters, and we need an end a result, in order to split the competitors

**EARTH** the time the climbers have to solve a boulder or a route is limited: the infamous Here and Now.

**WIND** we need to entertain an audience, so the show needs to be exciting, dramatic, anything but boring.

**FIRE** walls, volumes and holds are ever changing.

As route setters, we have not only to deal with these four elements, but in my opinion, we also have to play with a fifth, by introducing something... spicy, funny, beautiful, intriguing, different...

I don't have any specific words to explain what I mean. You can read all the books about cooking but in the end the main difference is this element of surprise you're able to mix in your own preparation, the one that will transform a basic recipe into a magical tasting dish.

## First steps : Some of the best and worst 5th elements in the past

From my experience, I can give practical examples of *fifth elements* introduced in past events. They are in the order of appearance since the beginning of competitions more 25 years ago, the letter B indicates bouldering events and L is for lead.

- Two lead routes with a shared section (that had to be climbed up by the women and down by the men without any changes between rounds. (L)
- Down climbing moves before it was forbidden in the rules ( B)
- Finishing a boulder in a bat hang (B)
- Playing with unknown holds, building our own volumes (B and L)
- Transformation of known holds in to new ones (with additional holds inside or changing the grip, we filled pockets with resin for example...) (B and L)
- One move boulders before the introduction of bonus holds ( B)
- A clock sequence in a section of moves (L)

- Hanged on feet (B and L)
- Climbing facing the audience (B)
- Parkour moves (the mimicking of street games) (B)
- Double or triple dynos (B)
- Run and jumps (B)
- Starting a boulder standing on two hands feet on the wall (for an invitational... out of the normal rules) (B)

I probably forgot a lot....

Why do I say "best and worst ?" Easy answer, each time you propose new things, climbers dislike them because it's an uncomfortable situation for them and they prefer to play in a familiar playground. Sometimes an idea can be good but it's not the right time to introduce it into the game. Finally, each new dimension needs to be carefully connected with the appropriate degree of intensity to the proposed situation.

I would like to develop two of these elements, one which was a success and the second one a failure, in order to demonstrate that we are on the razor's edge when we introduce any new element. But it is also exactly for that reason that it is so fascinating to be a route setter.

## CLIMBING FACING THE AUDIENCE:

We had this idea for a bouldering comp. The basic idea took a long time to adjust but worked pretty well in the end, except for the fact that, without any additional information given to the climbers, they probably would have spent most of their time trying to understand how to start. So I contacted the head of international judging to ask him if it would be possible to add an indication to the markings of the starting position to indicate right and left hands. After some discussion he agreed to my proposal, the boulder worked very well and it has now been included in the international rules.

## Downwards jump moves

During the same period, we had this idea to propose the first downwards jump during a bouldering competition, it was not forbidden in the rules at the time so we tried to propose a very impressive one which engaged the crowd. It was not hard to do, but it was hard to take the decision to do it; ultimately it was so intimidating that most of the climbers didn't even want to try it. It's interesting to note that all the climbers that did try it did it on their first or second try.

After the comp, one of the climbers wrote an article about this "*crazy dangerous moves that should be banished*" and few months later, downward jumps were forbidden in the rules.

## Thoughts

I will always remember this sentence I read in a famous French newspaper after a very big competition in Bercy around 1998 (I was not a route setter yet but a competitor): "As exciting as watching a painting dry".

It stayed with me and I have since always tried to play with the paradox between a pragmatic result for competition and idealistic vision to make climbing look more alive.

Undeniably in a competition, we need a ranking, we also need entertainment; and for that, imagination and creativity are essential.

And I like to think that it's much better to get a souvenir, some kind of flavor from an event, than just a routine. Nothing could be worse than this!

As it's becoming pretty hard to imagine new moves (I didn't say impossible!), we have to try to play with:

- Climbing structures, to consult with wall builders to get adapted walls for competitions (from slabs to overhang and everything in between)
- Specific holds adapted to each discipline (boulder or lead routes)
- Volumes

- Mental processes: risk to succeed on certain moves, creating doubt from the climbers
- Aesthetics (the audience's point of view)
- Create more and more complex situations for the climbers to solve
- Create a connection between climbers and audience

The last point is in my opinion the most important one because in our sport the climbers have their backs to the crowd 95 percent of the time, and it's very hard for spectators to perceive the effort in the muscles or doubt in the eyes or face.

So whenever the opportunity arises to create this rare connection through any climbing situation, I always try to vigorously encourage it.

## So, what's next ?

It is not for me to pass judgment on what's good and bad, I'm only able to give my opinion about the strict application of the rules by setters in the future. If we limit our jobs to getting a clear ranking, we might solve the problem of becoming an Olympic discipline but on the other hand we'll loose a lot of flavor inherent to our sport.

After 20 years of experimentations, is it still possible to find and propose new *5th elements*? The answer is in the hands of route setters.

For my part, I am already thinking of new ideas for the next competitions I will set for. Success or failure? The torture of it never ends!

# Jackie Hueftle

Jackie Hueftle began setting at Rocksport in Reno, Nevada, in 1998. Since then she has set for many large competitions including multiple USAC Junior Nationals and Pro Bouldering Opens including The Mammut Bouldering Championships and The Battle In The Bubble. She is currently the Head Route Setter at The Spot Bouldering Gym in Boulder, Colorado.

# The Importance of Mentorship

By Jackie Hueftle

I began climbing in 1998 at a small gym in Reno, Nevada. I was luckier than most—the gym paid their routesetters and had not one but two excellent setters currently on staff. These two, Bill Kelly and Ted Welser, made a practice of not only setting routes but of studying climbing movement. It was important to them to teach climbers to climb better intellectually as well as physically as they challenged them with their routes. This interest extended to experimenting with their own abilities and techniques down to the fractional turn of a hand or foothold.

Often with Bill and Ted routes there was specific beta that was necessary to climb the route well, to climb the route smoothly, and sometimes even to climb the route at all. They were strong enough, both had climbed at least V8 and low 5.13, but neither was some superman. Instead when setting difficulty they focused on the intricacies of movement. To help the gym clientele better absorb the lessons they were trying to teach with their routes, they created an affordable series of 4 workshops—Footwork and Balance, Bouldering and the Backstep, Resting, and Route Reading. At these workshops climber after climber became enlightened as to subtleties that lead to an advanced understanding of basic movement and better climbing overall.

I was lucky enough to take the workshops, then to be invited to a setting clinic that Bill was giving to introduce some of the gym's newer employees to setting. The clinic began in our favorite Pho restaurant, where we talked theory, then continued into the gym where, in pairs of two, we set our first routes. My partner was my good friend and fellow youth team member Patrick Cassiday, our wall was a toprope corner. I will never forget the moment when Bill reached the transition between the part of the route I'd set and the part Patrick had set. Bill stood there, stemmed out in a small dropknee in the corner, and twisted to look out at us and say something. As he looked out the hold he was holding and both holds he was standing on spun simultaneously. The rope was not super tight, so he dropped a few feet into the corner, spinning on the toprope and getting fairly scraped up. Patrick and I stood, mouths open, waiting to be yelled at. Instead when he stopped spinning he turned to us calmly. "Let's talk about properly tightening our holds." He said.

My learning experience was unusual in other ways as well. We set with hand wrenches, and the t-nuts at that gym in Reno were so good that for the first two years I didn't even know what a tap was. We got one eventually, but I don't remember ever using it. The gym was made by Radwall, the t-nuts all high quality, 3-screws, the fronts nearly flush with the gently textured surface of the wall. In retrospect it is one of the best and strongest wall-manufacture systems I've seen. The wall panels were so flat that it was easy to demand precision footwork, so, with the help of the gym's resident genius handyman (Steve Glotfelty, also the inventor of the original Hang Dog rope bag), Bill and Ted shaped five or six directional footholds they liked, made a mould, and started pouring. The result was a small quiver of technical feet useful in almost any situation without ever becoming easy or boring.

## Comps!

The yearly competition was a time of great excitement. For the first couple of years I was still a junior, competing in the comps, so I wasn't allowed to help set but I could come in the day before and strip and wash holds. The setters would set all night, and, supported by strong coffee, open the doors for registration in the morning. An air of great excitement surrounded comp day. A long redpoint round followed by an onsight lead final for the top six competitors. Finalists were allowed to pick their own music. The comp was followed by a free bar-b-que and live music.

Finals were always a blast. I remember one year the men's final looked like 5.11—every hold was a jug. Instead, because of the 1-foot-per-move way the route was set and the steep wall it was set on, the route was bodily exhausting and encouraged climbers to waste strength and power. Many competitors were shocked to pump off before they were even half way up the wall. The top competitors fought their way to the top, one falling two moves from the anchors and the other just below for a thrilling finish.

## New Ideas

Another time, long after Ted had moved away to pursue a PHD in Seattle, he returned for a weekend and graced us with a hard 12 up the steep lead wall. One move was a forced double bump with the right hand with your body sideways 2/3rds of the way up the 45 degree wall—a move that up until that point I'd never seen and, even when I did see it, didn't totally believe was possible.

## Finding the Flow

What I think made the setting so great was not just that the setters were particularly conscientious of movement, but that the way in which they selected holds and set with them encouraged climbers to make the correct movement choice and discouraged wrongheaded attempts. A common mistake in early setting is only being able to see the route going one way—the way the setter intended. To try and force the sequence an inexperienced setter will resort to tricks like not adding enough feet or picking worse foot or handholds. Unfortunately, the result is often that the route becomes less fun—awkward or painful even—and instead of the setter forcing people to do their weird movement people will choose not to climb the route. Alternatively, a good setter can work with the holds to encourage a climber to climb a sequence because the sequence not only works, but it is the easiest and best choice for how to do the problem. If you think of it like a river, water will flow the path of least resistance. Climbers will nearly always do what they think is easiest. Good setters can teach movement because they will encourage newer climbers to want to do the sequences they set. Those sequences will feel comfortable and natural, and if the climber doesn't figure it out for his or her self, a simple demonstration from a coach or a friend can often give them that ah-ha! moment that will show them the way through and forever improve their climbing in the process. For the strongest climbers it is the same—they will chose the sequence that feels easiest for them—and the solution is the same as well. Good setting directs the climber towards the intended path. This is not to say every climber will climb every route the same, but if the sequence and flow is solid, most will choose a very similar way of solving the problem, and that should be the path the setter intended.

Learning to set this way takes time, and if the setter is being paid, the time investment for a new setter to problem-solve their own routes can mean it is not equitable for the gym to pay the setter to learn. The solution in my case was a fixed rate per route—I'd get paid 3 hrs per route and I could work on it as long as I wanted after that but would not get paid more. This system allowed me to explore possibilities, to take as long as I wanted to set the route I wanted, without affecting the payroll adversely. In fact, I think this system had a positive effect on the gym overall, as my routes were better and I became a better setter overall because I was allowed to learn as I set instead of being expected to quickly churn out what would have been mediocre routes. Experimenting with movement is one of the things that keeps setters interested, and too many meat-and-potatoes routes = bored setters = a worse product.

## Learn Your Own Strengths

Early on in my setting there was a period where I would set very technical routes, often with high feet for perch/balance moves. I remember watching a member I knew struggle with one such move. "Just put your foot up and sit on it!" I offered. He couldn't figure it out, and I couldn't understand why. Later that day Bill took me into the front room and had me stand facing a wall from about a foot away.

"Touch your foot up as high as you can on the wall," he said.

Now, I've never been particularly flexible. I'm barely able to touch my toes and haven't ever done a split in my life. For some reason, and probably greatly helped by my girl's hips, I was able to touch my foot quite high on the wall from that standing position.

"Now watch me." Bill said. He was a much better climber than I, and technically far superior, but he could only get his foot to about 2/3rds of the height that I had. He then got a bunch of other guys from the gym to take the test, and all had a similar or worse result. Now I understood why my "easy" perch move was so difficult—the turnout offered by the typical male hip is far inferior to a woman's, and perch moves, instead of feeling like a cheating rest, were instead cruxy.

The lesson, that what is easy or natural for you will often be difficult, even awkward, for others, is one that I've learned and taught over and over. This is one reason I feel a consensus is important on an indoor route, and when other setters feel a problem I've set is harder than I think it is I often defer to them, assuming that as I set to my strengths the problem must really feel more challenging for them.

## Helping Newer Setters Set Well Means HELPING Them

Bill went on to teach me many many more lessons and help improve my setting, and he learned a thing or two himself in the process. For the most part his manner was calm and helpful—he focused not on me being "wrong", but on helping me understand conceptually what the gym needed and what a good route for the gym would consist of. He wouldn't change my routes, he would work with me to help me change them and understand the why. He also helped me learn to work through the stubbornness inherent in all setters—the feeling that the head setter is making you change your route because they don't "get it." What Bill helped me understand is that it doesn't matter if he gets it, it matters if it works for the gym and the customers, and if the head setter feels it is inappropriate for the gym, it should be changed. For this to work properly there must be mutual respect—that is, the head setter must hold him or herself to the same standard. If the other setters all feel a head setter's route needs to be changed, he/she should respect their opinion and comply.

So that's it. Good mentors mean the system works, the setters learn, and the gym, climbers, and setters all benefit. Good luck!

# TONDE KATIYO

Tonde Katiyo began climbing in 1984 in Zimbabwe and has been route setting since 1995. He believes in placing people and movement at the center of the setting process. His setting is an iterative, collaborative process in which forerunning and tweaking are key steps. In 2009 he formed a collective of like-minded setters : L'Ouvre-Boite providing high-quality setting and training services for gyms, competitions, and federations all over the world. Tonde has set for national and international climbing events throughout Europe, North America and Asia. In 2011 he was a guest speaker at the IFSC Route Setting Course on the topic of creativity in route setting. In 2013 he accepted a full time position as Head Setter of the Seattle Bouldering Project, but continues to grow his skills and love for setting through international jobs. He likes hip hop and good sushi and has a beautiful 2 year-old daughter.

# Risk Complexity & Intensity

By Tonde Katiyo

Since the beginning of climbing, people have needed to grade climbs. For some, to have an idea if the climb they're about to attempt is within their ability, others to assert that their newly bolted (yet unclimbed) route is (for sure) the hardest line in that area. Love them or hate them grades are an integral part of climbing culture, and are one of the true benchmarks of rock climbing accomplishments.

Then there is plastic. Statistics for gyms are on a steep upward curve : size, height, number, staff, membership, number of holds, routes… Inspiration for these man made climbs came from outdoors, starting with imitation of real rock and evolving into the flat surfaces with holds and volumes we know today. The grading system also made a meaningful shift as climbers went from estimating (arguing) how hard a rock is to climb, to making up climbs that should be a given grade; it's not a stretch to say : making up grades. And this in different gyms, in different countries, with different scales.

However, as climbing grows, where it is becoming an increasingly big deal is in competitions. As a route setter, I have set for many, and as I understand it, the main object of a competition (aside from show & promotion) is to find out who the best climber is at a given event. My job as a route setter is to set as fair a playing field as possible. In my attempts to achieve that, I have concluded that grades are just not a very accurate measure of objective difficulty in climbing making them a poor tool for route setters to communicate.

In 2009 I started a project that required storing as much descriptive information about a single competition boulder as possible in a database in order to serve as a resource and do statistics on later. I wanted to be able to communicate with a few precise words, the essence of a boulder.

I was, and still am a firm believer that in climbing many types of moves or styles should be represented. So I started by trying to list a finite number of styles and categories that could serve as a classification for all boulders. Styles included things like : physical, compression, technical, balancy, jumps and the categories had stuff like : type of holds, wall angle and grade among others. It turned out to be very hit and miss. Some boulders fell perfectly into a few neat words, while others would end up described as style : mixed, holds : mixed (or I also encountered holds : none), wall angles : mixed… resulting in a very vague and sometimes even ambiguous descriptions.

My research revealed that the creativity of route setters was challenging my definition system the same way it has been challenging the rules of competition climbing since its beginnings, forcing them to morph and broaden options or refine parameters. Deep down I was pleased that even under scrutiny, climbing was this ever changing unquantifiable substance, an endless combinations of human sensations, that had been a driving force and passion in my life. But I still felt frustrated that I couldn›t clearly articulate certain specific concepts about it.

I decided to consult, I sent out emails, raised the subject with other setters around me, we all seemed to agree that it must just be about finding the right combination. But two master route setters Jacky Godoffe and Laurent Laporte gave me key elements to put me on an altogether different —and I think— far more interesting track.

Laurent Laporte was the first setter I ever met to use a computer spreadsheet to design his competitions circuits. He used his computer both to plan before the competition and keep track of the advancement of his work during the event. He set up columns to detail the characteristics of a boulder such as location on the wall, setter, state of advancement or grade. At regular intervals during the setting he would gather the team of setters and the spreadsheet would provide a support for conversation and exchange, and he had a constant overview of his work. Nothing extraordinary about using a spreadsheet, but it was new to me, perhaps what validated it's use too, was how Laurent's amazing setting skill inspired me.

Jacky and I had worked together many times in diverse setting related jobs. I knew he voluntarily shied away from using grades when he set, other than to indicate a very general target grade to setters who are unfamiliar with a particular level of competition. He resorted to using a series of arrows, inclined at different 5 angles like the needle on a dial, to indicate 5 levels of difficulty, or intensity. What I really like about that system, is that the level of difficulty was relative to the particular category you were setting for. In youth events the same boulder used for 2 categories would get a different arrow level.

In a phone conversation with him I mentioned my dilemma in trying to describe boulder problems, and he told me about a scale to analyze individual moves with risk, complexity and intensity values. I knew of the terms and how he defined them, but I guess I never paid enough attention to their significance.

## Intensity – of extreme force, degree, or strength

In the context of setting and climbing I chose to understand intensity as the amount of physical force needed to do a move.

## Complexity– not easy to analyze or understand; complicated or intricate

How obvious (or not) the easiest solution to a given climb is, 1 being a very simple and straight forward problem and 5 the most cryptic.

## Risk – a situation involving exposure to danger.

I don't refer to danger in the sense of physical bodily harm but rather failure. Just falling on the rope or the mat. Risk defines how difficult a move is to control or the degree of commitment required to do a move. The higher the risk factor the lower the chance of success. For example an awkward sideways jump to a blind bad hold over a lip would constitute a very risky move. Adversely, moving a hand from one hold to another with 3 solid points of contact : completely safe : risk factor 1.

So I combined Laurent's and Jacky's ideas along with some of my own and began recording all the information I thought relevant about boulders in the various setting jobs I did in various countries. One part of the information was related to logistics such as name of the setter, location on the wall, category the boulder was designed for, order they were to be climbed in or color of holds or tape. The other part was to try and define very specific characteristics of each boulder, in the context of the event it was being set for, so : risk, complexity and intensity, then number of intended tops, number of actual tops, stars, number of moves.

The grid is a wonderful analytical tool, and the regular use of the spreadsheet revealed that the 3 particular parameters, risk, complexity and intensity were particularly accurate both to describe and adjust the difficulty of a boulder. This new scale solves many of the issues I had as a setter and instructor, because it allowed me to verbalize and quantify very specific attributes of a climb. But it doesn't replace grades, in a way it refines them. Where grades give an overall gage of how hard a problem is the risk-complexity-intensity scale measures how difficult it is. Semantics, but important distinctions to me.

In practice, when I plan a competition I now make conscious decisions about how risky, complex or intense I want a particular round. I'll give each boulder a rating for each parameter and then keep an eye on those numbers as the setting and tweaking gets done, as well as the averages for the whole circuit. It's still very empirical, but it works for me. The style column is still in my spreadsheet, and I continue to try and refine it, because it's descriptive nature will never be replaced by just 3 numbers.

The system applies well to commercial setting too. I use it to analyze the nature of the climbing in a gym and also keep track of how diverse the climbing product is across different grade ranges.

It is still a subjective system, the same way grades are. I can say Risk : 4 and another setter will call it a 2. It is what it is, but I like that we have words to put on the ideas we disagree upon. Healthy communication between setters is a key element (maybe the key) to good setting. The detail with which setters are able to express their climbing ideas in words should also transfer to how sophisticated their work and team work can be. Anthropology says so.

I'm nowhere near done experimenting with this new vocabulary, but I wanted to share what I have so far. I am aware that it is still imperfect, but hopefully by sharing it, others will improve it.

# Moses Potter

Moses Potter has been route setting since 1997. From 2007-2012 he managed the route setting program for Planet Granite. Currently residing in LA, Moses brings his unique perspective on route setting to Sender One Climbing, where he is the Head Route Setter.

# A Modern Perspective

Moses Potter

Route setting has evolved considerably since I first began in 1997. At that time, the holds were heavy, the work hard and thankless, and often I worked long days in total isolation. Washing holds could be an all-day endeavor and involved exposure to some pretty nasty chemicals. Thankfully, since that time, holds have become more ergonomic, durable, and colorful. The power tools of the trade are lighter and easier to use. Even washing holds, with the latest methods, has become much less onerous. Taken together, these advances, among others, have helped turn route setting from an entry-level, post-high school job to an honest-to-goodness *profession* or *career*. But even with these changes for the better, the core tenants of good route setting have remained constant: the joy of creating fun, thoughtful, and addictive movement, and the importance of the relationship to one's customers.

Modern climbing gyms face challenges gym builders of the past could never have imagined. For today's route setter, one challenge in particular can and must inform every aspect of his performance: the influx of mainstream crowds ("crossover customers") alongside the more traditional, diehard climbers. Crossover customers are the fitness- and activity-minded folks equally at home in a 24-Hour Fitness as they are in a full-scale climbing gym. Many crossover customers climbing endeavors will never take them beyond the plastic holds of their local climbing gym and onto real rock; climbing indoor routes is the end, and not the beginning, of their climbing goals and experiences. They want clean facilities, colorful, inspiring routes, and friendly interactions with employees.

To be successful, route setters need to embrace—rather than ignore or avoid—the needs of crossover customers. Adapting to the challenges posed by the crossover customer, modern route setters need to incorporate more nuance and subtlety into their craft—more footholds, smaller moves, and less intentional sandbagging, for instance. Likewise, routes that incorporate large features, "natural" wall features, and lateral movement can prove more popular than straight shots to the top of the wall; and, moreover, inspire a route setter to create more interesting, puzzle-solving movement. In short, route setters should capitalize on the opportunities to craft creative and comfortable movement allowed by the progression of route setting technologies and demanded by the challenges of appealing to a broader audience.

Perhaps the most important transition a successful commercial route setter must make is a mental one. Like chefs in high-end restaurants, route setters must understand that they are neither working for themselves, nor route setting to indulge their own personal whims, despite the inherently creative nature of their work. This is a tricky mindset to reach and maintain, even (and sometimes, especially) for the seasoned route setter. A route setter is at his best when he is creative and engaged; but at the same time, a route setter's work is just one aspect (albeit a vital one) of a successful gym. A route setter is an employee as much as the front desk staffer, and is accountable for providing a consistent product that reflects the standards and demands of the facility where he works. If a route setter produces work that does not meet the facility's standards, he needs to understand that the work will and must be changed, whether by the route setter or his supervisor. Therefore, and not surprisingly, any route setting program must have clear and definable metrics for measuring the quality of routes and boulder problems.

The concept of quality control may run counter to more traditional beliefs about route setting. Route quality has for a long time been understood as almost purely subjective i.e., a route that one person considers good is not necessarily good to another person. But most climbers know that this actually is not true most of the time. There is a reason certain routes and boulder problems at outdoor climbing areas get more traffic than others – because they are objectively better – better movement, better features, etc. There is a difference between subjective and hard to describe. And route setting is actually closer to the latter, not the former. As a result, while difficult at first, there is no good reason why a route setter cannot have quality standards in mind while going about his work. He has those same standards in mind when deciding what to climb himself.

Ultimately, like any group of people working together, a climbing gym company is greater than the sum of its individual parts, and is no stronger than its weakest part. In other words, route setters should consider themselves part of a team, working together to create a total product that is there for the public to enjoy. And as part of a team, route setters must incorporate accountability, consistency, and dependability as well as creativity into their craft – meaning quality standards are both unavoidable and indispensable. A route setter needs an understanding of quality so that he will not take it personally when his work is critiqued or changed. And an experienced *head* route setter must maintain and communicate objective quality standards consistently to all of his crew while simultaneously fostering their creative expression within those standards.

Since the public – both the crossover and the diehard climber – are a route setter's primary audience – not himself – a route setter must listen to the public's opinions of the work, and be able to accommodate their concerns. While climbing gym patrons often lack the language of setting and climbing movement, a good setter will interpret what his customers are saying when they critique the route setting (and they WILL critique the route setting), discerning what they are really requesting in their critiques, rather than just reacting to what they might be saying and dismissing it altogether. On some level, all climbers do understand what is good and what is not, even if they cannot express it. It is a vital part of a route setter's job to translate that criticism – and incorporate it into his work. Eventually, and this is the most difficult step, what transforms a good route setter into a great one is the ability to anticipate his customers needs and find the balance between satisfying and surprising his customers so they come back again and again, but are still challenged.

# Tyson Schoene

Tyson Schoene is the head route setter for Vertical World, Inc. He is also the head coach for the Vertical World climbing team. He's been setting since 2000 and coaching since 2002. Tyson has set for close to 100 competitions and acted as Chief Setter for dozens including quite a few Regional and Divisional level events. He has 0 USAC setting certifications.

Here's what Tyson had to say about his setting and climbing:

I have been climbing since the mid 80s. My family has been in this for a long time. I competed in the late 80s and early 90s, before taking a break and returning to climbing full bore by 2000 - I love this.

I've brought up a handful of young setters including Bret Johnston and Ross Halverson. I focus on mentoring young climbers to become well rounded career setters. We need more folks who look at this as a career path and take it as seriously as that. I don't want folks who set to pass time. I don't want to waste my time. I realize this isn't for everyone, but for those who want it - I will take the time to help them get there. I love my job. I am thankful every day for it. I get to work with kids and provide the community with climbing - it's hard to ask for more.

*Mesa RimKids*

# Thoughts When Setting For Children

by Tyson Schoene

Here is what I think about when I'm setting for kids:

Let me mention, that every day I set I set with little ones in mind. Working with kids for as long as I have has made me a much better setter. I feel it has given me an understanding of all body types and sizes. We have a ton of kids who climb in our gyms and we have a very large team. They need to be able to climb the routes without reach issues - every route from 5.8 to 5.13 needs to be done by sub 5-footers. Also, we have really short members who do not like to bend their arms past 90 degrees, so every time I set I keep the kids, and older ladies (who I love and are some of my favorite people – it's my job to make them happy) in mind. No one wants to set a reachy route. The "R" word is something we as setters need to take seriously.

## #1 Know Your Subject

A huge mistake people make is they think they know how little kids climb or they think that by bringing holds closer they are setting for little people. This is never the case. If you don't know how little kids or smaller members (keeping in mind these two climber types climb very, very differently) climb or what they look like on the wall, you will not be able to set good routes for them. I've been to dozens of comps where the setters, who are not coaches, say they have set problems for kids. Then you see a bunch of VBs and a couple crimpy ass V5s. Take some time to study youth climbing. If you are not a coach, sit at your team's practices to watch them climb. Recognize their movement and how they get around "reachy" problems. Look at the high-end kids and the low-end kids. You cannot guess on these things as the kids will always surprise you and come up with stuff you will never think of in climbing.

## #2 Never Be Afraid To Add Extra Feet

By adding a bunch of little feet you are not making the route easier necessarily, but it will make the difference between a 5-footer being able to do the move on a V5 and them not being able to get off the ground. I often put a row of 3 feet in an upward arc to give the option for all sizes. You would be surprised how far apart you can put the hands if the feet options are not limited. I've seen quite a few times where the shorter, stronger climbers getting hosed because there weren't extra foot chips added to routes. It doesn't hurt the route; honestly it is often more aesthetically pleasing, so you might as well do it. Then you never run the risk of having set a "reachy" route.

## #3 Make Sure You Understand The Distances Between The Feet And The Hands

The old elbow to elbow trick works, but it isn't that simple. Kids can and will climb dynamically and they will lock off at their waist. They are used to this and they can pop to holds you never thought of, but the trick is to make sure it isn't easier for someone of height and harder for someone who is shorter. One example is to put a foot higher, forcing a taller youth to have to hike it up and get their butt out, and put the hand farther so the little one has to pop a little - making the move equally difficult for both sizes. If it looks too far away, there is a good chance it is. Err on the side of putting the hold closer and no one will complain.

## #4 HOLD SELECTION

Little people can hold things that bigger people can barely use for feet. Be aware of this. If you are trying to force a sequence (for short or tall climbers), make sure they are not just going to climb up the foot holds. I've seen half a route at a divisional competition get skipped by a little one climbing the foot holds. Using smaller, ungrabable feet are just fine for most little ones - they are light and can stand on most things. Also think about how much bigger a 1/4 pad crimp is for a sub 5-footer. If you don't want them to rest there - change the hold. They will camp out on anything they can, which is usually something bigger people cannot. They will match foot chips with their hands; in all seriousness, they will match anything. Big slopers are a problem when setting for smaller folks. Their hands are small, so sloping pinches are very hard for them to get their hands around and they can't get much contact on big slopers. Just be aware of it and set accordingly.

## #5 CLIPPING STANCES

You have to make sure the clipping stances are equal for shorties and tall people. At Nationals in 2011 there was a huge advantage for girls over 5'3" in regards to a particular clip. Taller ones could clip off a jug, smaller ones had to clip in the middle of the crux so they didn't pass the clip and get penalized. I always put the clip at my eye level, and I'm 6' tall, so this makes it always doable for anyone sub-5 feet.

Those are a few of my thoughts. I really don't think about it much anymore as I have been setting this way for years. All my route setters are coaches, and a few of them are veterans of my climbing team, so they all have the same understanding of what it's like to climb like a kid and they all have constant contact with the kids and are able to watch them climb their routes. We get instant feedback every day. Even if my setter isn't coaching the night after setting, they usually stick around to see how the members and the little ones climb their routes. Don't just set and go home. Watch and see how different people react to your routes. Understanding who you are setting for is the most important factor in competition and retail setting, but in comps you can't make mistakes. Understanding that can mean the difference between a crying kid and pissed off family, and a happy kid and family who praise your route setting.

# Pete Ward

Formerly a full-time route-setter, Pete Ward is the Director of the UBC Pro Tour and the Managing Partner for NE2C Productions. His company was the first to introduce large-scale portable walls to competition, the first to broadcast live online and developed the modern scoring system for bouldering competitions. Pete splits time between Northampton, MA and Lucerne Switzerland and continues to work to bring climbing and its history to the widest possible audience.

# Love of the Game

By Pete Ward

I wrote an essay for the first edition of this book about pride. Louie asked me to write about what I thought was most important in route setting. I thought about it and realized that while there are many, many important skills required to become a good route setter, none of them matter if they are not applied in the correct context. If the reason you're setting routes is to be a Master of Puppets, to implement Your Unique Grand Vision for Climbing or for any reason other than because you LOVE climbing, sorry mate, you're doing it wrong. Your routes will not translate well to other climbers and your vision won't come to fruition because it's not about climbing, it's about you. I pointed out that, as Marcellus Wallace said in the movie Pulp Fiction, "That's pride fucking with you". You gotta humble yourself and fight past it. Only then can you understand the experience that other climbers have on your routes and that's the perspective you need to learn and to improve.

Fast forward to the second edition and now if you're reading this book, two things are probably true: First, you're probably under 30 and you have no earthly idea who Marcellus Wallace is. Second, you probably want some advice a little more tangible to help you become a better setter; A desire which, while admirable, is still a need I'm not likely to fill. In the words of Simon Sinek, "I'm not here to tell you how, I'm here to tell you why." And even though Louie asked me to write a different essay this time, one about how to organize a climbing competition, the why remains the same whether it's turning wrenches or negotiating venues. If you want to be in this game, there is only one acceptable reason: Because you LOVE climbing. And the bigger the stage, the more that needs to be true. Love and not a passing fancy. In my case, as has happened for millions of other people, although probably not very many other climbers, I realized my true love in Central Park, New York City. Here's how it went down…

In the time since the first edition of this book, my company, NE2C Productions has run many climbing competitions. Some were hugely successful, some not so much. Our highpoint to date was The Eastern Mountain Sports Pro, the first ever climbing competition in Central Park, New York City. This event was years in the planning and according to the NYC Parks Department it was attended by over 20,000 spectators very few of whom knew anything about climbing beforehand.

The most interesting thing to me about the EMS Pro was the fact that the huge audience of non-climbers was also the single most enthusiastic audience I've ever seen at a climbing competition in my entire life. They were engaged, anticipated everything that was going to happen and exploded in a cheering frenzy when it did. Far from being confused about the nuance of climbing, they were enthralled by the simplicity of it. To see an audience of non-climbers so completely taken in by the sport I love was a brilliant revelation for me that made me feel tremendous about the future of our sport and I'll confess, I was surprised that climbing was so well received. So how did it happen? Excuse me, why did it happen?

From an event production standpoint, the EMS Pro literally took years to pull off. We negotiated the venue. We built a legal framework within which the event could exist. We negotiated myriad subcontractors from the wall builders all the way down to the guys picking up the trash and emptying the porta-potties. We negotiated partnerships with government and with local businesses. We sold sponsorship at levels never seen before in our sport. To pull off the EMS Pro we needed to lean on everything we ever knew about producing events and in some cases, put aside what we thought we knew until later. For example: Never mind routesetting, forget about wall building, forget about broadcast and lights and pads and medical and insurance and anything else relevant to organizing a competition… It turns out you need a permit just to drive a tractor trailer onto the island of Manhattan. And tractor trailers are kind of important if you want, say, climbing walls at your climbing competition. To say that pulling off the EMS Pro was complicated is to say that Alex Honold is good at highballing.

But in my view, while there were lots of specific details that needed attention and skill to address, ultimately the EMS Pro didn't appeal to non-climbers because of any one specific thing. It appealed to non-climbers for two simple reasons: First, any human endeavor done well is inherently attractive. And second, because climbing is amazing and we love it. That simple fact, our love of The Game, motivated every single decision we made, from which screw was turned where to the decision to run the competition in the first place. A fundamental love of climbing and what climbing represents was, and continues to be, our bottom line.

And if you want to run your own climbing competition, that should be your bottom line too. Don't get me wrong, love of The Game isn't enough by itself. You still need solid project management skills, an airtight work plan, a schedule that is set in stone, event staff, setters, whatever level of event production you want etc, etc… but without love of The Game, none of it matters, you may as well be a wedding planner, it requires all the same skills and it pays better.

And at the end of the day, the reason why you need to love climbing to run a good climbing competition is the exact same reason why you can't have too much pride if you want to be a good route setter: Your routes aren't about you and neither is your competition. They're both about climbing and climbing is bigger than any of us. If you set the perfect route and organize the perfect competition around it, the best possible outcome is that no one will have any idea who you are. If you do it right, everyone will remember the athlete who did the climbing at an amazing and unique moment in our sport.

The great moments in competition climbing live forever: Edlinger at Snowbird, Sharma winning the X Games, Woods & Puccio currently sitting at seven US National Championships each... And every one of those moments happened at an event where hundreds of people worked, volunteered and cared enough to elevate climbing in the best possible light. When you organize a competition, you're representing a sport with over one hundred years of history and some of the great accomplishments of the best climbers that the world has ever seen wrapped up in it. You're standing on the shoulders of many, many great climbers who came before you and who loved The Game enough to want to share it with other people.

Make sure you keep that history in mind when you write its next chapter, no matter how small that chapter may be. Whether you're running an ABS local comp or helping produce the World Cup itself, make sure you cross every T and dot every I, no detail should be overlooked. If you chose to create and manage a gathering of the best and brightest in our community or any community for that matter, you are choosing to lead that community and you need to be doing it for the right reasons. You are representing our sport in its most public moments possible.

Back at the beginning I told you that I'm not here to tell you how, I'm here to tell you why, and the why is simple: Because climbing is amazing and we love it. But since this is an instructional text, I will share the most important parts of how you organize a climbing competition: With integrity. With passion. And with a commitment that everyone who sees your work will know that you and the sport you represent come from a grand tradition of visionaries who walked off the beaten track and into the mountains in search of adventure. Because climbing is art, climbing is honest and because climbing is amazing it deserves the highest respect from those of us who seek to elevate it. You're writing the history of our sport. Write it well.

# ROUTESETTER PROFILE

Identifying your personal strengths and weaknesses is an important part of accurate setting. It's also the first step for anyone trying to improve, as it shows the areas most in need of progress. The following profile worksheet should be filled out as honestly as possible. No matter how good a setter thinks they are, no one is good at everything.

If you are a Head Routesetter using this profile to determine the abilities of your team, do not just stop at having the setter fill one out on themselves. Assemble your team as a group. One by one have your setters leave the room and fill out their profile. In their absence, the remaining team members should collectively fill out a single profile on that setter, documenting the consensus opinion as to that setter's abilities. This should be performed for all setters (including you). As the Head Routesetter you can compare both versions and if necessary record a third profile showing your assessment of all the information. It's a good idea to keep a file on your team members and to have regular progress reviews (as with any other job). Update the profile sheet at every review, or if you notice ability gains (or losses) from time to time. The information reflected on the profile worksheet will help you to make better and more appropriate setting assignments and see where you might have holes in your setting team.

For your convenience the profile worksheet has been laid out in this book in such a way that it can easily be enlarged and/or photocopied. Feel free to do so and to use this worksheet however you see fit.

# ROUTESETTER PROFILE

## NAME: ______________________________

## DATE: ______________

### CLIMBING ABILITIES

Bouldering Level: Onsight ______ After Work ______

Route Level: Onsight ______ After Work ______

### ACCURACY SETTING ABILITIES

Bouldering: Lowest Accurate Rating _______ Highest Accurate Rating _______

Routes: Lowest Accurate Rating _______ Highest Accurate Rating _______

### CLIMBING STRENGTHS:

*1 = Weak* *2 = Below Average* *3 = Average* *4 = Above Average* *5 = Strong*

CRIMPS______ PINCHES ______ POCKETS______

SLOPERS______ UNDERCLINGS ______ DYNOS ______

GASTONS ______ BODY TENSION ______ CAMPUSING ______

Power Problems (2-6 moves) ______ Stamina (6-12) ______ Endurance (12-20) ______

### SETTING STRENGTHS:

CRIMPS______ PINCHES ______ POCKETS______

SLOPERS______ UNDERCLINGS ______ DYNOS ______

GASTONS______ BODY TENSION ______ CAMPUSING ______

Power Problems (2-6 moves) ______ Stamina (7-12) ______ Endurance (12-20) ______

# Angle Strengths:

*1 = Weak* *2 = Below Average* *3 = Average* *4 = Above Average* *5 = Strong*

| | Climbing | Setting |
| --- | --- | --- |
| SLABS | ________ | ________ |
| VERTICAL | ________ | ________ |
| 10 – 20 degrees overhung | ________ | ________ |
| 20 – 35 degrees overhung | ________ | ________ |
| 35 – 50 degrees overhung | ________ | ________ |
| ROOF | ________ | ________ |

Other than the facts on the first page, I feel that I am a strong coursesetter because:

(what I do well) ____________________________________________

____________________________________________

____________________________________________

____________________________________________

____________________________________________

____________________________________________

____________________________________________

Other than the facts on the first page, I feel that I am a weak coursesetter because:

(what I want to learn to do better) ____________________________________________

____________________________________________

____________________________________________

____________________________________________

____________________________________________

____________________________________________

____________________________________________

____________________________________________

# COMPETITION MAPS

When setting climbs to be used in Semi-final and Final rounds of competition, it's often a good idea to draw a quick map of the climb. The map should always be made by (or with the input of) the person who set the climb. In this way, as much of his/her intentions will be portrayed on the map as possible. This map will serve as a written representation of your climb and will help the judge(s) assigned to the climb to better understand your intentions for the climb and the competitors climbing it. It also makes re-setting the climb much easier and faster if it needs to be removed from the wall for earlier competition rounds. Shown on page 196 is an example of a map showing a Finals round boulder problem. There are many things to keep in mind when drawing your map.

- Your map should contain any and all information that you consider pertinent to the climb, and any information that you feel would make the judge's job easier. This should include at a minimum the division the climb is set for, the round of competition, the difficulty, the point value (and any special scoring rules that might apply), and the name of the routesetter.
- All hand holds (including starting and finishing holds) should be shown clearly and drawn in such a way that they show the basic shape and orientation of the hold.
- While not shown on this map, you may want to write the color or manufacturer (or both) of the hold for further clarification, especially if several adjacent holds are similar.
- Show which hand the hold is intended to be used with by placing an L (left) or an R (right) adjacent to the hold.

- Unless there are other climbs set in the same area that overlap your climb, or unless there are specific foothold qualities that are important enough to be shown specifically, all footholds can be shown as bold dots on the map.

- Define the starting position (i.e.: sit start, crouch, standing, jump, run and jump, dead hang, etc.).

- Number the moves on your map in the order in which you intend them to be performed, not necessarily in the order in which they appear on the map. This sequence should be checked through the forerunning process and should reflect the easiest path through the holds. The first hold to be grasped after the starting hold(s) will be marked #1, as it signifies the first actual move of the climb (unless the route features a dynamic start, in which the target hold(s) would be labelled as #1).

- Intended hand matches count as two separate moves, and the hand that you intend to grasp the hold with first should have the lower number. It's possible that competitors will match on other holds during the climb, but unless these are matches that you deem to be probable and necessary for further progress they should not be numbered or count in the scoring of the competitor's effort on the climb.

- When judges use your map they should write the initials (or number) of the competitor adjacent to the furthest hold touched, controlled or moved from (depending on the scoring system used in your competition) to act as a representation of all competitors' efforts on the climb.

Another popular method of using competition maps is to either supplement the map with a color printout of a photograph of the problem itself, or to print a larger copy of the photo and to mark it up accordingly for use as the competition map instead of drawing a separate one. If you are going to do the latter, it's a good idea to print it lighter in order to allow for better visibility of the written notes.

## MENS FINAL #3

**V12 2000 Points**
**200 points per hold**
**Setter : Louie Anderson**

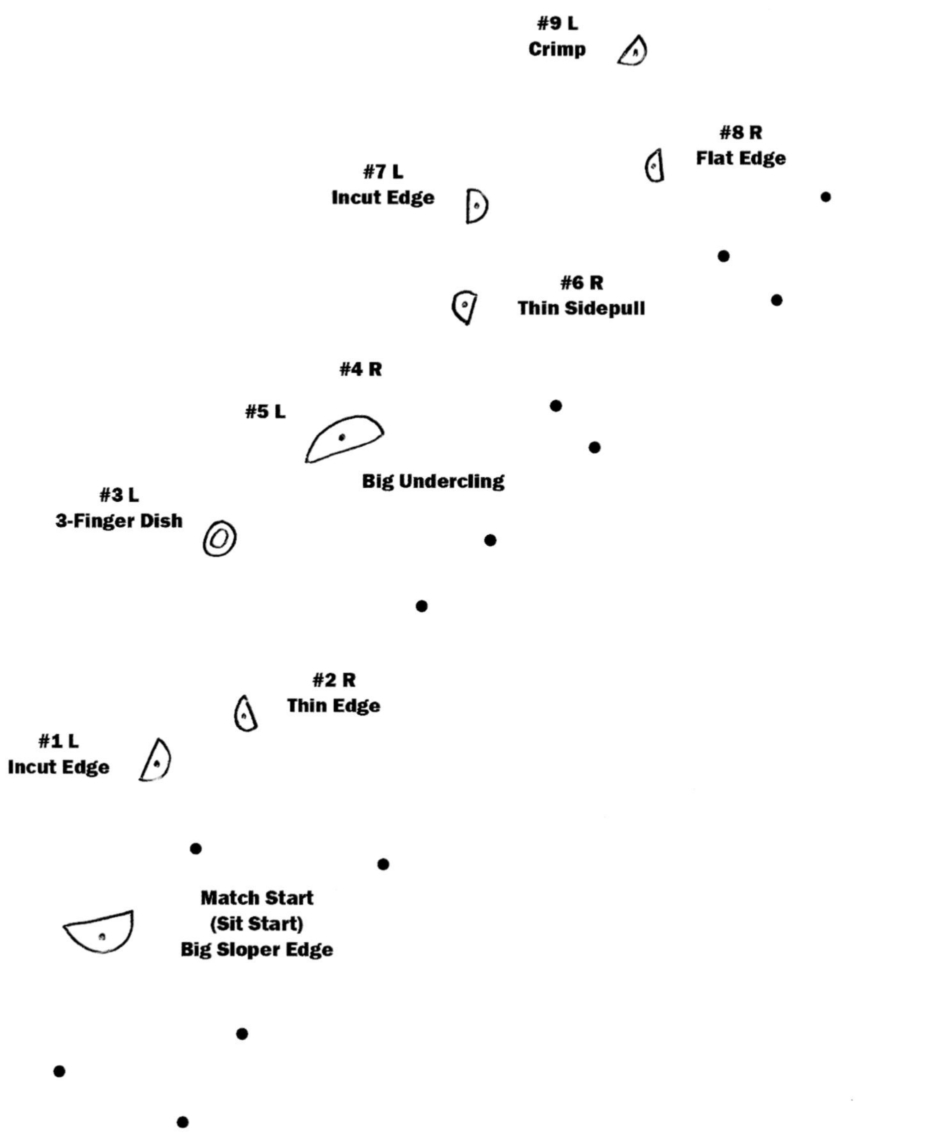

# ROUTESETTER EXERCISES

Once you (and your setting team members, if applicable) have completed the Routesetter Profile, there are a number of fun and educational exercises that you can participate in that will put you in a position to further explore what you can and cannot do by presenting a series of setting challenges. By going through these exercises individually and as a team you will learn more about the specifics of certain types of routeesetting and cannot help but learn new techniques and expand on what you already know.

Some of these exercises may seem silly or redundant at first, but all are designed to either reinforce what you already know and expand on those talents, or present you with a specific challenge. These challenges will help to expose the weaknesses in your own setting style and force you to learn how to overcome those weaknesses.

All of these exercises have been given to a wide variety of setters, with drastically varying strengths and weaknesses in the context of routesetting clinics. While some exercises will prove more worthwhile (depending on your current setting strengths and skills) all of them will put your setting to the test. By continually testing ourselves as setters, we improve.

# Individual Exercises

While the exercises listed below are designed to be performed by a single routesetter, many of them have a greater impact if another setter is used initially to select holds for the setter performing the exercise. All exercises should be performed with no outside comments, suggestions or other input until the climb is done. At this point, it's a good idea to open yourself up to critique (by climbers and other setters) of your climb. Try not to be offended by what you hear and use the comments as the lesson learned by the exercise. Once you have received feedback, do your best to fix whatever rough spots and errors might be a part of your climb. An important step in progressing as a setter is learning to recognize errors; the sign of true progress however, is knowing how to avoid and remedy them.

**Grab bag** – Select the number of handholds that you think will be required to cover the distance that your climb will travel. This exercise works best if you don't necessarily make an effort to select holds that are similar in size or style. Because you will probably do this anyway on some subconscious level, this exercise is often done with a partner selecting the holds that you will use. Place all holds in a big bag or container that cannot be seen through. In addition to these holds you will need a wide variety and size of footholds. To start the exercise you reach blindly into the bag and select a hold. No feeling around; whatever you touch first is the hold you use. The hold you pull out becomes the starting hold. Repeat this process with each hold pulled being the next handhold used on your climb. The setter is allowed to use any size, style and quantity of footholds he/she would like to in order to coordinate the pulled hand holds into a climb that "flows." This is a great exercise to work on handhold orientation and foothold selection.

**Draw Three** – Write many different wall angles that are found in your gym on slips of paper (slab, vertical, 20 degree overhang, 45 degree overhang, roof, etc.). Place them all in a jar. Do the same for difficulty (easy, medium, hard) or (5.8, 5.9, 5.10, etc.) and place these slips in a different jar. Finally, do the same for hold type (pinch, edge, crimp, sloper, jug, etc.) and place these slips in a third jar. Pick one slip out of every jar for your setting assignment. Once the jars and slips are made, they can be kept for future use.

**Focal point** – Select (or have another setter select) a large, unique hold or pair of holds (it's best if the selection does not represent your strength or usual style). This selection will become your focal point. Place it in what will be the center of your climb, with no real attention paid to the orientation of the hold(s) when installing. Set a climb around, and complimenting, the focal point. On longer climbs multiple focal points should be selected and installed prior to beginning the "fill in" setting. A simple exercise that reinforces sequencing, both into and from key moves or holds.

**Spin setting** – This exercise works best if another person does the initial spinning. If this is not an option, it will still work OK if done by the setter performing the exercise. To start a random selection of holds is picked and used (in a random order) to mark points of progress along the path of the intended climb. The holds are installed on the wall with a sizable gap between them. When setting boulder problems they should be installed 5-10 feet apart from each other. For setting roped climbs they should be installed 8-15 feet from each other. When installed the hold's mounting bolt is tightened until the hold is not quite touching the wall surface. The hold is then spun on the mounting bolt. Whatever position the hold stops in is the orientation in which it should be tightened. When using holds that are long and do not spin evenly, select a random orientation by stopping the spin with your hand. Try to put some variety in the spacing of your spun holds. This means to not just install them in a vertical line. Allow the line to wander a bit to the left and right as you move upward. The setter now needs to select any additional hand holds and footholds he/she desires and link the spun holds into a cohesive climb. The only real rules are that all spun holds have to be used (not just as intermediates or "bumping" holds), and used in the intended order. Because the spun holds will not seem that far apart, this is a great exercise to learn sequencing, setting up for specific movements and the use of directional holds.

**Set strengths** – Based on the results of your Routesetter Survey (see page ???); set a climb that matches your strengths. The only catch here is that you should set either **far below** or **far above** (or a climb of each) your normal setting level. This exercise allows the setter to stay in a style of climbing that is comfortable, but forces him/her to step outside of their usual difficulty range and challenge the skill to set at that level. Critique by other setters and climbers (that are comfortable at those levels) will determine if the setter met the challenge or not. Once the initial feedback has been received, the climb should be adjusted however necessary with the help of a setter comfortable with that level of setting.

**Set weaknesses** – Based on the results of your Routesetter Profile (see page 191); set a climb that matches your weakest scores. This should include both hold type and steepness. To begin with it's OK to stay at a difficulty rating that you are comfortable with. As you continue to perform this exercise start to move away towards whatever grade is more difficult for you to set at (easier or harder). Again, the critique of those more comfortable with this style of climbing is important and the climb should be adjusted with the help of a setter more proficient with this style.

**Speed Setting** – Just what it sounds like. Set a time limit roughly equal to 1/2 the amount of time it would normally take for you to set a given climb. The clock starts after the holds have been selected and when the first hold is installed on the wall. Stop setting when the time runs out (regardless of whether or not you have finished) and critique yourself on what you would have done differently given more time. When repeating the exercise, continually adjust the time limit (as you get to where you can set quicker) to where you don't quite have enough time to finish the climb. For safety reasons, this exercise is best performed when setting boulder problems. The benefits here mainly revolve around becoming more efficient and seeing and selecting movement and hold options quickly and accurately.

Finally, go to other facilities and sample the routesetting that they offer. Ask yourself what their team of setters does differently than you. Is it better? Worse? Why? Whether the trip teaches you some new sequences or reinforces what you are already doing, the trip will have been worthwhile.

## Group Exercises

Many of the individual exercises can also be done as a group. Some of the following exercises can take a little time to do properly, but make great excuses to get your setting team together and learn from each other or boost team morale and cooperation. If your team has regular setting meetings, this would be a great time to work on an exercise or two. These exercises are usually led by the Head Routesetter.

**Alpha and Omega** – Before starting, three good sized piles of hand holds need to be separated (each pile should have about three times the number of handholds required to set a climb on the given section of wall, and offer many different sizes and styles of holds) and placed at three different sections of wall (preferably of differing angles). Split the whole group into three smaller groups, with each assigned to a different section of wall. Each group will set the first 1/3 of a climb on that section of wall using only holds from the pile designated for that section of wall. Once all groups are done (to increase the intensity of the exercise set a time limit in which to complete the 1/3 to be set) they will switch wall sections. After this rotation they will set the **final** 1/3 of the climb (again only using handholds from that wall section's pile of holds). The groups will then rotate to whichever wall section they have not yet set on. This is where the real challenge of the exercise comes into play. Selecting hand holds only from whatever holds remain in that wall section's pile; the group must set the missing middle 1/3 of the climb. The goal here is to flawlessly link the lower and upper thirds into a climb of the same style that transitions nicely from section to section. Any number or type of footholds can be selected by the team as needed to incorporate into their sections. On a truly successful climb the point where the thirds join will not be noticeable to other climbers. This exercise is great to develop team setting skills, spatial skills and for developing the skills necessary to set climbs that truly "flow."

**Tag team** – Split the whole group into two smaller groups. Each group will select ten hand holds for the other group to use. The groups will take the selected holds and set the first six hand moves using only holds from the original ten selected holds. The groups will then select another ten hand holds for the other group to use. Again six hand moves will be set, choosing holds only from the ten selected holds (holds from previous selections are no longer an option). This continues until the two climbs have been completed. The groups will then critique the other group's climb. A variation to this exercise has the groups switch climbs at each ten-hold selection, back and forth. This variation limits the group's ability to plan ahead and anticipate possible future sequences on their climb. Once again there are no limitations placed on the number or style of footholds used. Hold selection and conservation become important during this exercise, as each hold placed on the wall limits the options for the next hold to be used.

**Add-on** – Similar to the popular bouldering game, each setter is responsible for setting a certain number of moves, followed by the next setter providing the same number of following moves. When setting boulder problems each setter should provide 3 hand movements. For roped climbs each setter should provide 5-8 hand movements. If the whole group size is quite large it would be best to split it into small enough groups to allow for each setter to have more than one turn on a given climb. Each climb should be critiqued by the group(s) at the end of the exercise. The benefits of this exercise can be exaggerated by mixing the smaller group's setting strengths and weaknesses.

The exercises listed represent a small number of possible exercises. Feel free to combine elements of any and all of them to create new exercises. The important aspect of these and other exercises is to put setters in an unfamiliar setting environment, often with existing components that are out of their control, and challenge them to set a good quality climbs. Forcing the setters to rise to the challenge (whether or not true success is found in the resulting climb) is the underlying motive.

The group activities are also a good way for team building to occur and something along these lines should be scheduled at regular intervals throughout the year to provide a fun and safe environment for everyone to come together and improve as a team with shared ideas, support and encouragement. Perhaps couple the activities with a team meal to follow to allow for further bonding and development of the team mentality.

# DYNO COMPETITIONS

BY TY FOOSE

Due to their crowd-pleasing, gravity-defying leaps and dramatic catches, dyno competitions have become more and more popular in the past few years. From freestyle acrobatics to World Record distances, there are many different formats for dyno competitions, but the most exciting include a wide variety of the many different styles of jumps. Following are definitions that apply to dynos and descriptions of several jumps that you can set. Like tricks in skateboarding, many of these can be combined, refined, or expanded to make some really impressive dynos:

**360**- Launch, and then spin a full 360 degrees in mid air before grabbing the target hold

**Atomic Drop**- Target hold is significantly lower than the launch hold requiring an all-points-off drop

**Brickyard**- Also called run-n-jump, not to be confused with the Slam Dunk. Running at the wall and kicking off of a foothold to launch to the target hold

**Courthouse**- Landing position requires grabbing with at least one hand and an opposing toe hook

**Criminal-** Launch, then spin 180 degrees or more by using multiple steps on footholds before reaching the target

**Double Dyno**- Grab the target hold with both hands simultaneously

**Dropkick**- Swinging or dropping to land on a distant foothold

**Dyno**- Any dynamic move where no more than one limb remains in contact with the launch holds when grabbing the target hold

**Font Start**- Jump from the ground to the target hold using a handhold to help generate the vertical leap

**Gap**- Launch from a wall and spin 180 degrees to grab a target on an opposing wall behind you

**Hill Glide**- Swing one arm back, and then swing it toward the target hold using the weight of the arm to generate upward momentum

**Jumper**- Climber who practices dynos often

**Ralston**- Launch using only one arm and grab target hold with the same arm

**Reverse**- Grabbing the target with your back to the wall

**Second Generation**- Using an intermediate target hold to help carry your momentum to the final target hold. The intermediate hold is usually too sloping or hard to hang on to on its own.

**Second Step**- Launch, then step again on one or more footholds to reach target hold.

**Slam Dunk**- Jump to the target from the ground without kicking off the wall and without using a launch hold. May or may not require running start. Not to be confused with the Brickyard or Font Start

**Sprag Landing**- Target is 2 separate holds spaced apart from each other

**Superman**- When your full body swings out to a horizontal position upon grabbing the target hold, usually done on very overhanging walls

**Target**- Finishing hold or holds, finishing position, or destination

**Tarzan**- Usually a sideways second generation dyno where you grab a first target hold and allow your momentum to immediately swing you to a second target hold

**Tension Grab**- Grabbing the target requires body tension, most common when the target hold is an undercling or is on one side of a corner

# COMPETITION ORGANIZER CHECKLIST

**2-6 Months Prior**

- Hold initial organizing meeting with the head setter, gym manager and comp organizer
- Contact and secure sponsorship
- Contact local/regional media

**Month(s) Prior**

- Finalize all event schedules, format, etc
- Finalize sponsors
- Design, print and distribute promotional flyers/materials
- Post volunteer sign-up sheet
- Contact local/regional media

**Week(s) Prior**

- Begin route-setting
- Meet with volunteers, judges and other staff
- Finalize pre-registration
- Print t-shirts
- Contact local/regional media

**Day(s) Prior**

- Finish route-setting and fore-running
- Label problems
- Print scorecards
- Hang sponsor banners
- Setup sponsor display table/space
- Stock-up on registration and scoring materials
- Contact local/regional media

**Comp Day**

- Coordinate registration
- Pre-comp rules talk (rules, scoring, sponsors, exits, spotting demo)
- Announcements throughout comp
- End comp and collect scorecards
- Distribute food and drink
- Process results
- Throw finals or dyno comp??
- Prizes/award ceremony
- Party??

**Post Comp**

- Post and distribute results
- Thank sponsors
- Re-set the gym

*Gabe DeWitt*

# ADVERTISERS

Please take the time to look at the following advertisements. The companies represented by them have chosen to support this book project and further the development of routesetting in general. If any of them in particular is of interest please contact them or go to their website using the information provided in their advertisements. I thank them for their support and hope that you will do the same by considering and purchasing their products.

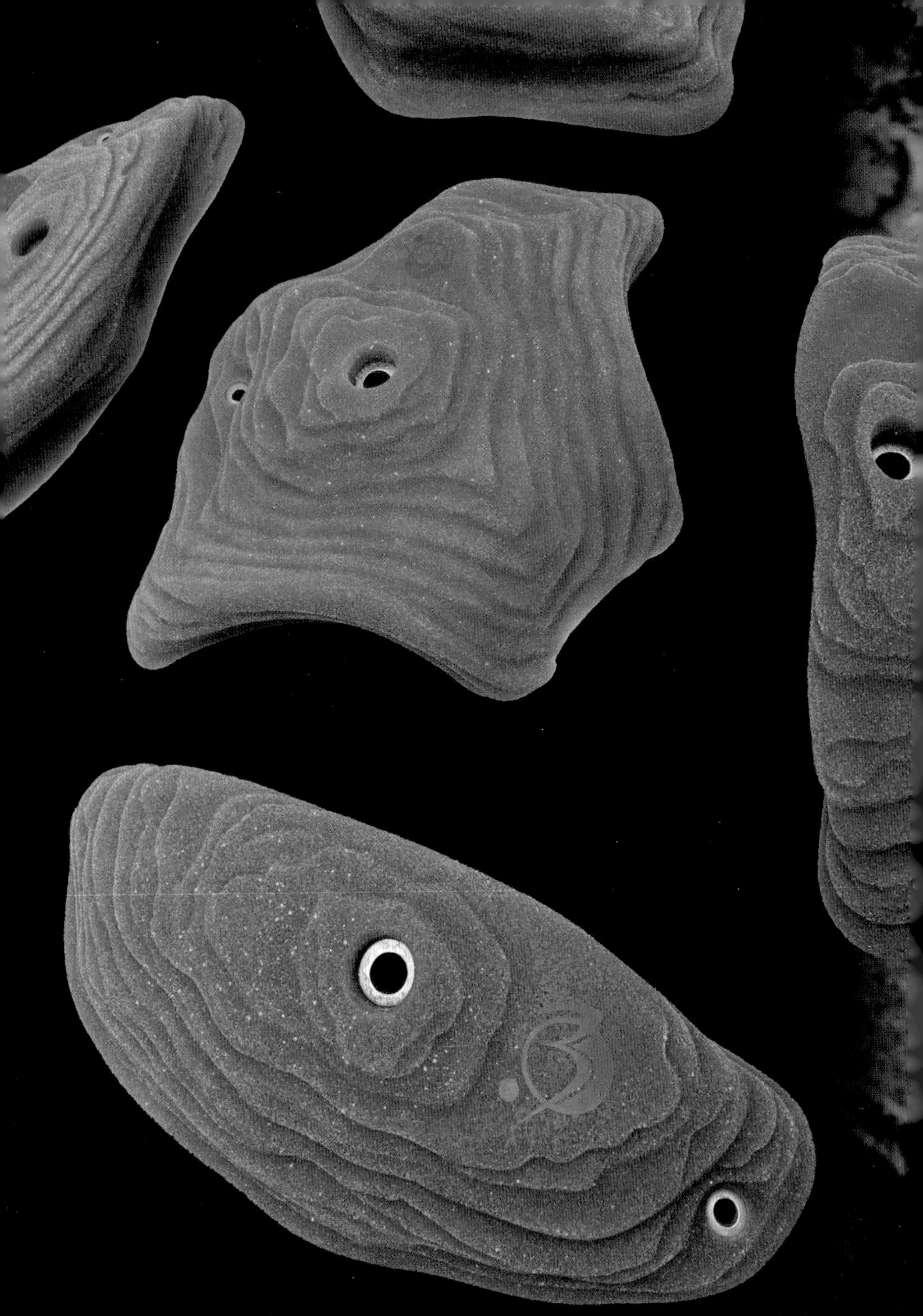

Tortuga con Tortuga...

Three Ball Climbing

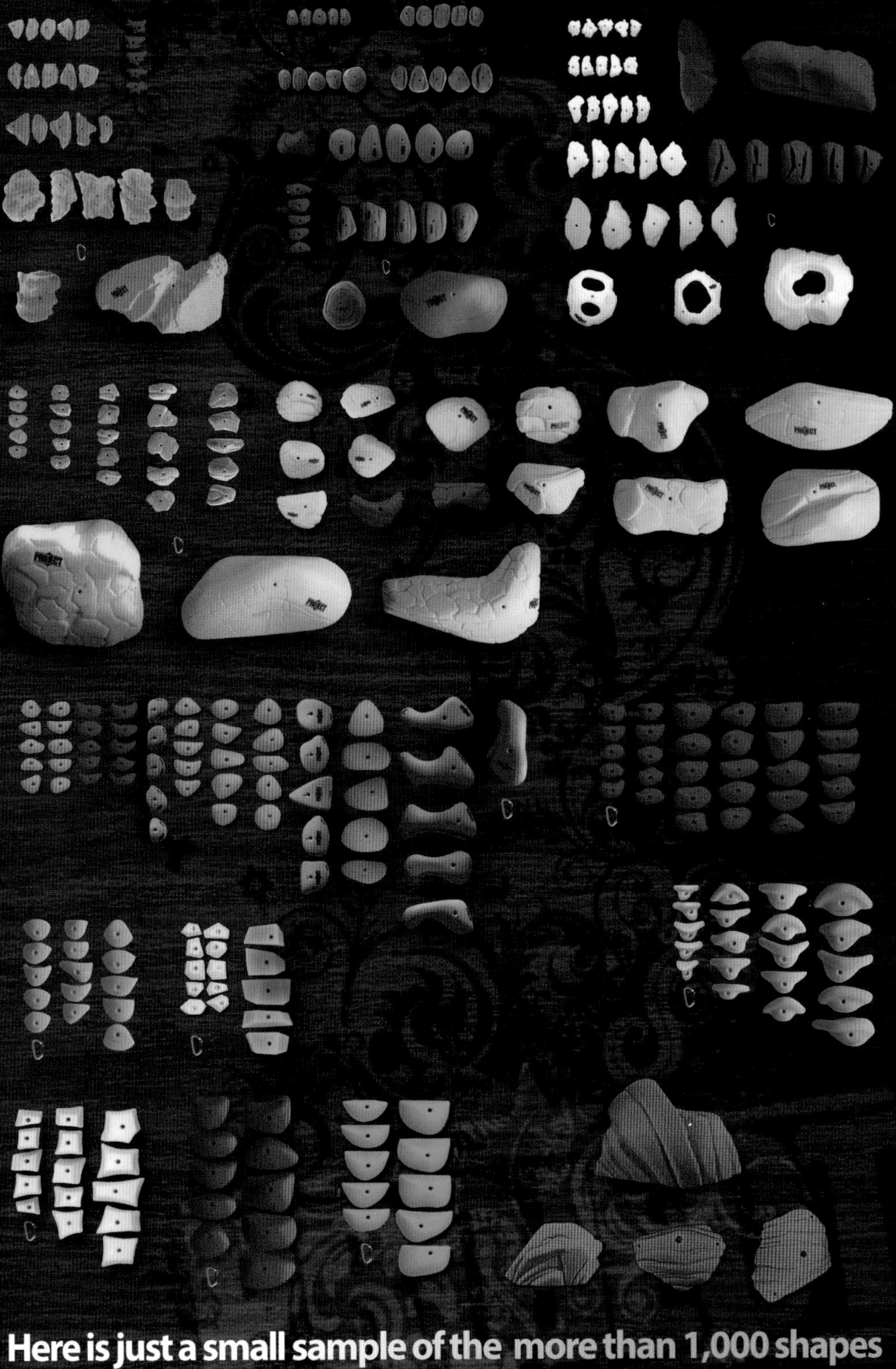

**Here is just a small sample of the more than 1,000 shapes in our arsenal, with several brand new series, features, and volumes on the way.**

ADD SOME VOLUME
TO YOUR CLIMBING
WITH DELIRE'S
EXCLUSIVE ANCHORS
délire
prises d'escalade
delireholds.com

Photo by route-setter Ryan Jones,
from Earth Treks Climbing Center
in Rockville, MD.

Ec
Element Climbing
Element Climbing
World Class Urethane Climbing Holds Since 2008
elementclimbing.com

CAPITAL
www.capitalclimbing.com

REACH FOR ATOMIK.
Route artistry when your canvas is blank.
UNBEATABLE
UNBREAKABLE
GUARANTEED
ATOMIK
CLIMBING HOLDS
atomikclimbingholds.com

ESCAPE
ROCK CLIMBING HOLDS
DESIGNED
by routesetters
FOR routesetters
escapeclimbing.com

PRINZ
CLIMBING HOLDS
www.prinzclimbingholds.com

USA Climbing is a 501(c) 3 not-for-profit organization that sanctions and hosts over 200 climbing competitions a year. As the National Governing Body in the United States for Competition Climbing, USA Climbing is recognized by the International Federation of Sport Climbing, the International Olympic Committee, and the United States Olympic Committee.

**www.usaclimbing.org**

PHOTO BY TIM KEMPLE
Featuring Iron Palm
LIVE IT.
OWN IT.
So iLL
www.soillholds.com | wecare@soillholds.com

Only Mother Nature Makes Better Shapes.
ETCH

# ABOUT THE AUTHOR

Louie Anderson is a lifelong climber and is actively involved in all aspects of the indoor climbing industry. He's been routesetting since 1987 and has been very active in the Southwest region of the US, setting for high-end competitions. Louie is also the most prolific freelance hold shaper in the world, having had more than 10,000 of his designs commercially produced since 1988. Aside from his setting and shaping experience, he owns his own climbing wall company, installing everything from garage "woodies" to high-end, sculpted concrete commercial gyms. In 2012 he opened his own bouldering gym, The Factory Bouldering, in Orange, California. The Factory is the largest bouldering only facility in Southern California and provides the local community with an excellent training and social resource.

Louie is married to his best friend and climbing partner, Valarie, and has two daughters. The Anderson family lives in a rural area of Orange County, California, in a home that they built themselves.